HOW TO WORK
WITH SELF HELP GROUPS

To Clare and Jon

The Joseph Rowntree Foundation has supported this project as part of its programme of research and innovative development projects, which it hopes will be of value to policy makers and practitioners. The facts presented and views expressed in this book, however, are those of the author and not necessarily of the Foundation.

How to Work with Self Help Groups

Guidelines for professionals

Judy Wilson

arena

© Judy Wilson 1995

Published by
Arena
Ashgate Publishing Limited
Gower House
Croft Road
Aldershot
Hants GU11 3HR
England

Ashgate Publishing Company
Old Post Road
Brookfield
Vermont 05036
USA

British Library Cataloguing in Publication Data

Wilson, Judy
  How to Work with Self Help
  Groups: Guidelines for Professionals
  I. Title
  361.7

Library of Congress Catalog Card Number: 95 - 80523

ISBN 1 85742 288 0 (paperback)
ISBN 1 85742 289 9 (hardback)

Typeset in 10pt Palatino by Jim McLean, Nottingham. Printed in Great Britain by Hartnolls Ltd., Bodmin.

Contents

About the author

Judy Wilson has worked with and written about self help groups since 1982. She combines voluntary sector management, training, consultancy and research. She holds a M.Phil. degree from Loughborough University and in 1990 was a Senior Research Fellow at the John Hopkins University in Baltimore, USA.

She is the author of *Self Help Groups: Getting Started, Keeping Going* and *Caring Together*, two practical handbooks on running self help groups and carers groups and has written many articles and reports.

She has lived in Nottingham since 1970. Since 1982, she has been Leader of the Nottingham Self Help Team, the leading local self help centre in the UK, and since 1992 its Research Director. Judy is a Non-Executive Director of Nottingham Health Authority. She has travelled widely, having visited or worked in Africa, America, Canada, Australia and both Western and Eastern and Central Europe.

Acknowledgements

I would like to acknowledge the help of a wide variety of people and organisations who contributed both to this book and to the research which led to it – and to thank them all.

- Members of self help groups and professionals working in the Trent Region who took part in the research and national organisations who contributed their views at a seminar.

- The Joseph Rowntree Foundation for supporting the research project and Tessa Jowell MP and Dr. Janet Lewis for chairing the project's advisory group.

- Dr. Jill Vincent of Loughborough University for her professional advice and Mai Wann, Jane Bradburn, Glenda Taylor and Fiddy Abraham, and again Jill Vincent, as members of the advisory group.

- Colleagues in the United States and Canada for their insight and time, especially Andy Farquharson of the University of Victoria and Lester Salamon of the Johns Hopkins University, whose fellowship programme led to this subsequent research.

- My colleagues in the Nottingham Self Help Team, especially Angela Dobie for her administrative help.

- Venture Press, British Association of Social Workers, for their willingness as publishers to allow some of the contents of my research report *Two Worlds* to be adapted for use in this book.

- Dr. Nori Graham, Cyril Ible, Anne Kelly, Rosemary Carpenter, Judy Young and Janet Williams who read drafts and helped so much with the process of distilling a wealth of information and opinions into practical guidelines.

Abbreviations

AA	Alcoholics Anonymous
A & E	Accident and Emergency
CPN	Community Psychiatric Nurse
CVS	Council for Voluntary Service
GA	Gamblers Anonymous
GP	General Practitioner
OT	Occupational Therapist
ME	Myalgic Encephomyelitis

Section one

Setting the scene

1   Introduction

Coping with loss, ill-health and change are part of everyday life. Most of us get through or learn to cope with help from family and friends, often finding that the best support and information comes from those of them who have already gone through a similar experience. We ask for and largely appreciate professional care at times but it is only part of the help we need.

Self help groups are another way of getting and giving help. They provide a further form of support when help from family, friends and professionals is not enough, is inappropriate or not available. A competent professional recognises the value of self help groups, wants to work with them and is prepared to learn the best ways to do so. This book aims to help individual professionals working in health and social services to assess, extend or change how they work on a day-to-day basis.

It is written for people working in both statutory organisations – health service and local authorities – and in large voluntary organisations. It is intended to be useful for a wide range of professions: social workers, health visitors and other community nurses, doctors in general practice and in hospitals. Psychologists, occupational therapists and physiotherapists, dieticians, speech therapists and counsellors will also find this book relevant to their work.

Research

How to Work with Self Help Groups is based on experience, not on theory. During 1992–4 an in-depth research project was carried out in the area covered by the then Trent Regional Health Authority, supported by the Joseph Rowntree Foundation. Using qualitative methods, interviews were carried out with a

3

wide range of professionals and members of self help groups and the literature was reviewed *(Wilson 1993, Wilson 1994a, Wilson 1994b, Wilson 1995)*.

As the research on which this book was based was carried out in England, titles common in England are used, readers in other parts of the UK being asked to adapt any specifically English names or structures to those used in their part of the country.

This book uses this recent research but also draws on my wide experience of research, development work and training with groups and professionals over ten years prior to the project. It has then strong roots, in both practice and research but the end product is my interpretation and recommendations – and should be read as such.

A working definition

The term 'self help group' is the one most commonly used in the UK today. Other terms can be appropriate – support group, user group, mutual aid group or mutual help group – but none of these are generally used and 'support group' is more appropriate for groups led by professionals. While 'self help group' does not entirely describe what these groups are, it is the term adopted. Five essential elements can be seen:

- Members share a common difficult experience in their lives
- Members own and run the group
- The people who come benefit from its activities
- There is some degree of structure and organisation
- Members may pay subscriptions or contributions, but not fees

A definition is needed too, rather just than a list of components. A definition adopted by the Nottingham Self Help Team, one organisation's attempt to draw some boundaries round its work, has been used as a working definition.

"A self help or mutual aid group is made up of people who have personal experience of the same problem or life situation, either directly or through their family or friends. Sharing experiences enables them to give each other a unique quality of mutual support and to pool practical information and ways of coping. Groups are run by and for their members. Some self help groups expand their activities. They may provide, for example, services for people who have the same problem or life situation; or they may campaign for change. Professionals may sometimes take part in the group in various ways, when asked to by the group."

(The Self Help Team 1993)

Taking this as the working definition has meant that other types of group and self help activities are not included here. This does not mean that they are not valuable and helpful but simply that the subject of this book is a particular form of group, and their relationships with professionals. Its focus is on the majority of self help groups: those concerned with a specific issue. Most illustrations and quotations come from members of groups based on health and social issues, these being most likely to be of interest to readers of this book.

Contents

The book is divided into three sections. The following three chapters that make up the remainder of Section one aim to set the scene, in Chapter 2 exploring the question of definition and how self help groups overlap with other initiatives and organisations. Chapter 3 examines why professionals might choose to work with self help groups. Attitudes and knowledge are important influences on practice: values and attitudes are covered in Chapter 4 and how to learn more about groups in Chapter 5.

The heart of the book is Section two, on ways to work with groups. Chapter 6, the most important chapter to read, explores how professionals can put people in touch with groups and how this differs from referral. Helping groups as they start and continue and promoting their work form the topics of the next three chapters, 7–9. Listening to what group members have to say, including hearing their views on professional care and services comes in Chapter 10.

Three chapters make up Section three, covering topics which have arisen earlier in the book but brought together here as common themes. Chapter 11 identifies different variables which are likely to influence how work might be carried out, and raises the need to work in ways which suit the situation and the people concerned. Dilemmas and challenges are summarised in Chapter 12, there being no magic solution to resolving them all. Finally, Chapter 13 encapsulates good practice, emphasising that both self help groups and professionals can benefit when relationships work well.

How to use this book

The intention is to provide a handbook which offers guidelines rather than a textbook to be followed slavishly. Checklists and summaries make it possible to dip rather than have to read it cover to cover. Readers should select and follow the guidance which is relevant to their profession and where they work – or can disagree and devise their own. This is new territory. There will be different opinions and other solutions to problems; debate and alternative views are welcome.

Leave them alone

The research findings made it clear that most self help groups wanted professionals to know about their work, to value it and to support what they did. Support, however, does not necessarily mean involvement. Self help groups occupy a very different world from professionals and actual professional involvement may in fact be the last thing a self help group needs. The most important ways of working with self help groups are putting people in touch with them and supporting them in public, neither requiring involvement, but needing knowledge and skills.

Leaving groups alone does not mean ignoring what they do. It is important to know how to contact them, understand how their help could be useful, and to value their contribution. This book attempts to help professionals explore these issues as much as how they can be involved.

Involvement is certainly not discounted altogether, for some professionals will become more involved, which can be right and proper and what groups want at the time. An approach which suits the group and the situation is best. A dilemma in writing this book was that in setting out the different ways in which professionals can work with self help groups, I could have been seen to be suggesting that methods were for all professionals and all groups. This is not intended: the different ways of working with self help groups are to be taken as options, not prescriptions.

But the best course of action may be in the end to leave them alone. Read on with this in mind.

2   Self help groups

This chapter explores what self help groups are. Stories of four self help groups provide snapshots of a variety of groups, introduce their distinctive flavour and illustrate some of their special ingredients. How self help groups overlap with other organisations with some similarities is discussed. I look at the range and scope of self help groups; some of the common activities groups undertake, and their benefits and their limits. The chapter ends by considering distinctions between self help as practised by an individual and mutual aid through self help groups.

Self help groups – some stories

Four accounts below illustrate some of the groups which form the focus of this book, not giving a full picture of the group but rather why a group feels important to the person concerned. Many of the issues they raise have a bearing on possible relationships between the group and local health and social services professionals.

Downs Syndrome Group   "I've been a member of the local Downs Syndrome Group for about four years, ever since we moved here. I'd been a member of another group where we lived before, so obviously moving up here we wanted to know what was available.

     We've got about thirty five people on the mailing list, but there's a core of about twelve to fifteen families. You usually find the same people come to meetings, other people just want to be involved for the social side of it. We make a point of not trying to fundraise because we think that takes away from what we want to do.

If you can see someone who has coped with the situation you think, well, they've managed it, why shouldn't I? If you're having a problem you know you've got someone to talk to who may have had a similar problem.

We tell people – don't go along to the library and read the books there, they're ten years out of date. Things have changed. But we try not to swamp people with information – you've got to give people time to think about the implications of it all.

Sometimes we write letters to the Health Authority, or to Social Services – we don't always feel they're providing the services we'd like. But most of us come for the support and the information."   *(Jo)*

Asian Single Mother and Children Group   "In our group the women are single, usually either divorced or widowed and have children and we are all Asian. They need someone to talk to and somewhere to go with their kids. We can use the creche at the Family Centre where we meet. They can ask for advice, they can just talk – and we go out together. We have lecturers in it and a social life as well.

I'm myself a single mother with three children, but I'm lucky, I have a car, I can drive, I can get out. But most of our members can't drive, they just sit at home. And being in an Asian society, they are not very accepted by that society.

Most of the women don't know where to go for help. They are scared to come out. We would like to put a stop to this, to make our women strong so they can come out. Sometimes they come first just on an outing, then they get to know us and come to the meetings.

I get a lot of satisfaction from doing this – if I make someone smile for about half an hour, I think it's worth it. I've been through it and I know how it feels."   *(Kaneez)*

Tinnitus Group   "I've got tinnitus – noises in the head – and I've got it very badly. The medical profession do try and relieve it but there's no cure of course. They will tell you to go away and live with it. They don't tell you *how* to live with it. They don't really understand the social and family problems associated with this disease. It's not life threatening of course, though people have committed suicide because of it. I've had to ring the Samaritans myself some nights.

I'm the secretary of our group. We meet once a month – I know some members would like to meet more frequently but it's a bit too much to organise. We try to get a speaker, it may be on tinnitus, but it can be anything which is a diversion. We advise people to keep themselves busy, so we always try and have an interesting speaker.

But we make sure there is time to talk as well. When people first come, they just fall on each other – just can't stop talking, telling each other how it is. Lots of smiles and lots of tears.

We help each other in the group and we raise funds. We raise funds for research in order to find a cure – that's our two objectives." *(Terry)*

Tranquilliser Support Group "We were put on them: 'These will do you good.' I was put on tranquillisers after the death of my Mum, but I wanted to come off so I went to the tranquilliser group. With their support, knowing they had been through it, I managed it. When I got better I felt that I wanted to share my experiences and let other people know there was light at the end of the tunnel. Lots of us have had a lot of help from professionals. There's a really helpful community psychiatric nurse for example. But we feel we're the ones who've been there.

It's not always easy – everyone should pull together in a self help group, but they don't always. There seem to be a few people who get things done while others sit back and drink a cup of coffee. And some people are still on tranquillisers and having enough problems just getting to the meeting. But it's not just the meetings that's needed. We have a helpline in the evenings and people phone each other up a lot.

We went to an event and the Mayor was there. The Lady Mayoress said to me – how are you trained for this sort of thing? *Well*, I said, for what I do I only need one sort of training and that's coming off Ativan." *(Elaine)*

Mutual aid in other settings

Chapter 1 set out the definition used as the basis for this book. While an author must say what a book is about, applying tight definitions is not the total answer. Self help groups can change and develop into other sorts of organisations and can overlap with other types of group. Drawing a blurred circle round self help groups and then seeing what other activities overlap with them helps deal with the dilemma of definition. Fig 2.1 illustrates overlaps with organisations with some similarities to self help groups, but which fall outside the definition used.

This book does not attempt to discuss how professionals can lead support groups, commission self help services or be involved with national self help organisations. It does not cover relationships with campaigning and advocacy groups or the intensive work needed for some forms of community self help. Seeing however their overlap with self help groups contributes to a total picture and adds to the process of defining self help groups.

Figure 2.1   Overlaps between self help groups and other organisations

Professionally led groups

Mutual support between people in the same situation is not unique to self help groups. It can take place in groups led by professionals as well as those run by their members. The difference is that in professionally-led groups, professionals lead the group, define its membership and purpose, and decide where it meets and for how long it will last. Members do not own the group, nor feel responsible for its operation. Professionals make a commitment of time and effort to attend and their work will be seen by their managers as part of their job.

Some professionally led groups may be described as support groups, often having fairly loose forms of organisation. Others may be better termed therapy groups. There can often be confusion in people's minds between professionally-run groups and member-run self help groups. It is important for professionals interested in working with self help groups to be clear on the distinction and to understand there are very different working methods in the two different types of groups.

Self help services

User-controlled services, increasingly starting in the mental health and physical disability fields, have some of the characteristics of self help groups but are not the same. In the mental health field they have been defined as projects providing services controlled and used by people who use or have used mental health services. Projects are controlled by everyday members of the project and are independent of mental health workers and funders *(Lindow 1994)*.

A variety of projects exist in this country, providing clubs, independent living support, housing and other services. The main difference from self help groups is that their primary aim is to provide services, though support and information often result as well. One major implication to be recognised is their need for consistently provided resources.

National self help organisations

National self help organisations can also have some of the characteristics of a self help group. A national organisation's management committee may be made up of people who have themselves experienced the problem upon which the group is based. Some, however, see themselves as more a medical charity, include medical and other professionals in their management and concentrate on research, education and fundraising rather than on mutual support.

In whatever way they are managed, the function of a national self help organisation differs from that of a local self help group. They are likely to have local groups as branches, or linked loosely with them, and to provide group services and opportunities for members of local groups to meet each other. They cover the whole country, not a local area.

A hybrid organisation can exist, for if a group is based on a very rare condition, it may operate nationally but members also try to give each other support and information. Phone support may be used if meetings are impracticable. A group may start as a local group and evolve into a national organisation.

Advocacy and campaigning groups

Self help groups centre on the needs of their own members and some deliberately stay with an inward looking focus, concerned with personal change rather than influencing society. For others, campaigning may become part of their range of activities, but not be a primary function. A range of other voluntary groups carry out campaigning for change, advocacy work with and for other people or aim to influence professional services and educate the public as their main purpose. These too overlap with self help groups, with their members getting support at the same time as taking action, but they are not the same.

Community self help

An even more difficult area to describe and summarise is what may be called community self help. People living in the same geographical area often get together and undertake activities from which they will benefit and from which the wider community will gain. A good example of this are playgroups, begun three decades ago from the initiative of parents wanting preschool activities for their children, and now a widespread movement with a strong national organisation.

Community self help may be informally organised. A group of widows living in the same block of flats may meet for coffee, help each other out when ill and share feelings of loss and adaptation to a life without a partner. They are unlikely to call themselves a self help group, and calling them this could over-formalise what may work best informally. Churches, temples, mosques and synagogues, particularly for people from black and ethnic minority communities, may also be the setting for community self help. Mutual support may happen as part of religious activity, or it may arise through groups sponsored and supported by the religious body.

The range and scope of self help groups

Having set self help groups within the context of other initiatives, I return to groups which do fall within the suggested definition. Their range and scope can be very wide. First, they vary according to the issue on which they are based and the list below summarises the types of group there are:

- Physical illness
- Disability
- Mental health and well being
- Addiction
- Carers groups
- Social issues
- Generalist support groups

Chapter 11 will go into more depth about the distinctions between these types. Within these broad fields there are other variables: groups for women, for example, are likely to be different from groups open to men and women and will raise different issues for professionals to consider. Groups for black people have a special focus and needs. How groups are organised can vary a great deal, meaning that any two groups, though based on the same condition, can have a very different feel and focus.

There are many other variables of which professionals will need to be aware and to take into account when thinking how they might work with self help groups. The list below summarises what issues can affect both how a self help group runs and what it does:

- The issue on which the group is based
- Whether it addresses a rare condition or a common problem
- The attitude of society to the issue
- Age range of members
- Number of members on the books
- Number of active attenders
- Members from one ethnic group, or mixed
- Rural or urban areas
- Working class or middle class areas
- Part of a national organisation or independent
- Frequency of meetings
- Length of time the group has run
- Closeness of relationship with professional services
- The degree to which members identify and value lay expertise

The variety of activities

Second, groups vary in what they do, as opposed to what they are. The accounts earlier in the chapter illustrated how all four groups provided support and shared information, basic activities found in all self help groups. Quite how these two functions, and others are carried out will depend on the group. The range of common activities found in many self help groups includes:

- Sharing experiences and information in small groups
- One-to-one support and befriending
- Hospital visits
- Telephone support
- Talks at meetings
- Library of books, articles and leaflets
- Newsletter
- Publishing handbooks and literature
- Social activities
- Fundraising
- Campaigning for change and educating the public
- Taking part in consultative meetings

Benefits and limits

Self help groups bring benefits from belonging, but they also work within limits. The following lists summarise how people, in groups and in the professional world, see these strengths and limits.

Benefits	Limits
Mutual support	Not right for everyone
Information	Personal limits of time and energy
Confidence raising	Limited group resources
Opportunity to be helpful	Difficult groups to run
Influencing services	Not valued and supported

Self-helpers often combine being perceptive about the limits to their groups and their activities with being assertive about the benefits they have gained from belonging.

"I think the main point is just meeting someone who has been through the same thing. People who haven't been through it just don't understand. A group is somewhere where people know they can say anything."

(Clare, Eating Disorders Group)

"You find out a lot more by going to a meeting. You can read hundreds of books on a subject but you can go to a meeting and someone will say something, perhaps just an off the cuff remark and it happens to relate to you as well."

(Jill, ME [Myalgic Encephomyelitis] Group)

"They've really boosted my confidence. They've re-educated me – I can go and talk to nearly anyone now. I'm a lot better chap than I was."

(Mike, Mental Health Group)

Professionals have another perspective. They see how people, who may also use professional services, can benefit by being in a group.

"It relieves people's anxiety – they meet people in the same boat."

(Ian, GP [General Practitioner])

"Experience sharing frees people up from feelings of responsibility and inadequateness."   *(Alison, Social Work Assistant)*

"I like it when my patients go to self help groups. When they come back to see me, we have a much better discussion."   *(Marion, GP)*

It would be wrong to paint a totally rosy picture, for there can be difficulties of many kinds. Like many small groups, self help groups may have problems and, as included in the list of limits, can be difficult groups to run. Chapter 12 explores further some reasons why sometimes self help groups do not work as well as they might.

The idea of self help

To end this chapter, professionals need to be aware of distinctions between the idea of personal self help and an actual self help group. Helping oneself is both part of individual change, which may be a solitary action, and of mutual aid in a group setting. Personal self help, as endorsed by Samuel Smiles (1958) nearly 150 years ago can work without a group and many people may well prefer such an approach.

In a self help group, self help is part of a collective activity, involving contact with other people. Almost a prerequisite of joining a self help group is the wish to do something for oneself. The additional dimension, not part of personal self help, is that of mutuality. The concept of mutual help – I help you, you help me, or you may help someone else altogether – is an essential part of a self help group. While individual change may result, it will be through a process of mutuality rather than through a solo approach.

Summary

- Being aware of definitions and key ingredients is the first step before starting to work with self help groups.

- There can be both overlap and some clear differences from other organisations.

- Professionally-led support groups are not the same as member-led self help groups.

- A wide range of self help groups exist, with many different variables influencing how they run, carrying out a variety of activities.

- Mutual support and sharing information are functions common to all.

- Groups bring benefits and operate within limits.

3 Why work with groups?

The intention of this chapter is to explore reasons for working with self help groups. Clearcut arguments for undertaking this work may not be apparent and questions as well as answers will be raised. Personal experiences and outlooks affect interest and approaches as much as professional influences. The aim is to provide a framework so that professionals reading this book can begin to assess their own personal motives for working with self help groups, and why their agency might do so.

After setting the context of this work, three broad types of reasons are explored: the first arise from valuing self help groups; the second come from seeing working with them as part of good professional practice; the third from self-interest. The last point includes the question of whether professionals might undertake this work as a means of exercising power and influence. A final checklist offers the chance to assess why one might work with self help groups.

Context

Looking at work with self help groups should be set against a context of current issues in health and social care. Community care policies in recent years would seem to have a general aim of maintaining an individual's links with family, friends and their own community through the provision of both informal care and formal services *(Reading, 1994)*. The implications of the 1990 National Health Service and Community Care Act are that self help groups have an important part to play as part of this informal care, and as one means for the voices of users and carers to be heard. Discharge arrangements have become crucial in community care and an Audit Commission report on hospital discharge proposed that information on self help groups should be part of the procedure *(Audit Commission 1993)*.

In the area of health care, the Patients Charter endorses the need for patients to have access to information. Setting up and funding regional healthlines, for example, has been one way in which the Charter has been implemented. By including self help group information in this service, central government would seem to accept the role of groups as part of broad policy.

Finally, the 1989 Children Act actually requires professional agencies to give parents information about services. No other specific strategies have been spelt out, but working with self help groups can be set against a background of some recognition, in general terms at least, of the contribution and importance of these groups.

Whether personal or contextual influences are stronger, professionals might decide to work with self help groups because groups are valued for what they are and what they do. It is this angle I shall first explore, reasoning that if one values something, one should logically take some action to support it.

From valuing self help groups?

Many professionals who work with self help groups do so because of a basic belief in the value of people doing something together, which is different from professional care. Appreciating the special contribution of self help groups can lead to taking action for a variety of reasons:

- To help groups become more effective
- To get more groups started
- To help people feel empowered
- To help people develop their potential

Helping groups become more effective

If one values something, one wants it to work well. Many people working in health and social services quoted in this book have been motivated, in part at least, by wanting groups to run better. Professionals who are trusted and accepted by group members may be able to help a group become more effective and to improve the quality of what they do.

There are dilemmas here: to what extent can a professional intervene in the working of a group? Can one do anything if advice is ignored? Could professional help have the effect of deskilling ordinary members? Chapter 8 discusses these and other issues in more detail and suggests principles on which work might be based.

There are difficulties for any outsider trying to help a group become more effective, but a professional thinking about why they might work with a group should also be aware of opportunities. They may be in a position to help a group become more effective in achieving its goals, and professional support may avoid someone struggling to reinvent the wheel alone. Practical support is likely to be perceived by group members as demonstrating that what they are doing is valued, so making them feel encouraged and more confident.

More self help groups

Helping new self help groups start is the subject of Chapter 7. Professionals involved at this stage may be doing so because they appreciate groups' contributions and see a gap in the support which users of their services need. Self help groups are valuable, so there should be more of them could be the argument here.

This approach also raises some questions. How far can a professional initiate a group? Can a successful group in one place necessarily be replicated in another? Is a health and social services professional the best source of support when a new group is starting? These and other issues – taking a role as a catalyst, for example – are addressed in Chapter 7. Raising questions like these is not meant to suggest that a professional should necessarily hold back, for they may be the only person who has an overview and can see the need. Lack of professional action may be as much of a constraint on the development of new groups as too much or inappropriate involvement.

There are two very different approaches to starting new self help groups: as a lone worker, or as part of an agency policy. It will be helpful to think whether any work undertaken is likely to stem from personal values and commitment, or whether it is part of the way an organisation works. Sometimes both may be influences.

Helping people feel empowered

A third aspect of valuing self help groups is seeing that they are a means of empowerment. There can be problems associated with this approach, for it can be seen as patronising, but professionals can help people to feel empowered, and to take control of part of their life.

Both individual and agency practice can again both be considered. The two may or may not coincide. If policies are based on principles of empowerment, then it will be easier for the individual worker to develop work with self help groups. An example comes from a local family centre.

> "The whole approach of the Family Centre is to help people get control of their lives, to regain their confidence. Encouraging the Asian Single Parents Group that meets here is part of our approach."   *(Ruth, Social Worker)*

Most professionals will be working in organisations which have adopted equal opportunities policies to a greater or lesser extent. Commitment to equal opportunities policies logically leads to valuing disempowered people doing something for themselves. As women, as black people, as people with disabilities for example, people in self help groups are seeking to empower themselves. Action by professionals to support self help groups may be a method of putting an equal opportunities policy into practice.

Recognising potential

Some professionals choose to work with self help groups from seeing potential in individual clients and patients. They have a talent for spotting the capacity people have for action and believe that people can grow and change. They recognise how helpful it can be to be helpful. Encouraging someone to initiate or become involved with a group, because they have something to give may be the reason for taking action.

Again there are risks and dilemmas. For example, could too much encouragement mean someone feels pushed rather than just encouraged to start a group? Too much concern about possible disadvantages nevertheless may mean opportunities are lost. Valuing self help means not only valuing what people can receive, but also what they can give.

Professionals may well have opportunities to encourage people to help – valuable for the individual, and important for a community. A social work professor in Canada with wide experience of self help groups, puts this in context.

> "In my view, there is still too much professional attention directed to the ill-health, weaknesses and incapacities of people and not enough emphasis on personal resources and abilities which can be the well-springs for personal growth and change."   *(Farquharson, 1990)*

Part of good professional practice

Professionals who believe in the value of self help groups may also work with them because it is part of good professional practice. One can look at this under a number of headings:

- Giving access to other forms of help
- A means to help prevent future problems
- A way to improve the quality of professional care
- One way to enable users' views to be built into plans and policies

Giving access to other forms of help

It can be regarded as good general professional practice to know about and use other sources of help in the community. Writing about health visiting, for example, Drennan outlines ways in which health visitors should develop a network of contacts in the community.

"It is only by developing these relationships that health visitors can begin to work with people in response to their own needs and tap into the resources and expertise of other organisations and disciplines."   *(Drennan 1988)*

A broad spectrum of practice exists. Some professionals see their job solely as providing professionally run services and no more. At the other end of the spectrum are those who put people in touch with other forms of help as part of their normal practice. People like this, natural networkers, recognise gaps and limits in their own services, and see their role as a link to other forms of help.

"We're always looking things up. We're very much brokers – always putting the work out to where it should be."   *(Alison, Health Visitor)*

Referral on to other forms of professional care is a well accepted part of good practice. Linking people to informal sources of help in the community, like self help groups, cannot be approached in quite the same way. This topic, putting people in touch, the term preferred to referral, is discussed in Chapter 6.

   Some professionals are very definite about the limits to their own services. They have no monopoly on help, as they see it, nor is professional help necessarily the only form of expertise. Some feel indeed that they would be very foolish not to make use of other people's expertise.

"We cannot set ourselves up as the be-all and end-all. There is plenty of room for real experts."   *(Clive, Rehabilitation Assistant)*

Part of the self appraisal of practice could be to analyse the extent to which networking and putting people in touch with other resources, generally, is a key part of practice. It can be assessed as an individual and from the point of view of agency strategy.

Prevention

Preventing distress and pain and avoiding inappropriate use of professional services are objectives many professionals would set themselves. Working with self help groups may well be a form of prevention and one reason why a pro-active approach can be important. Membership of self help groups can prevent some illness, prevent re-admission to hospital on occasion and avoid some inappropriate use of professional time. Being a member can also ward off isolation. The examples below illustrate these points.

Preventing illness   A mental health agency in a rural area which had had no large psychiatric hospital had assessed the philosophy for its work, resulting in developing and giving access to a safety net of support becoming an important part of its approach. One client, a woman suffering from intermittent depression, had been ill both before and after the new strategy had been implemented. She told a nurse how she much she valued the network of self help groups in her community, groups which had been actively encouraged and supported by the local Mental Health Team.

> "It's not just pills and someone going to see you once in a while, she said. There's now something on-going to prevent it next time."
>
> *(Dave, CPN [Community Psychiatric Nurse])*

Preventing re-admission   A nurse became involved in helping a cardiac support group. Talking about her reasons for doing so, she said she was sure that some unnecessary admissions to hospital in the past could have been avoided.

> "They were petrified when they were discharged. They came back in, sure they had had another heart attack, when all it was was twinges. I felt that if people could see others who had had the same thing, they would feel more able to cope."   *(Dora, Hospital Sister)*

Preventing inappropriate use of professional time   Good professional practice is concerned to make sure that specialist skills and time are appropriately used. A General Practitioner had encouraged a patient who had asked his advice to join a group for people with depression. She had had frequent appointments, not always for entirely relevant reasons.

> "She used to come and see me every week. But when she joined the group, she only came when there was something I could really help her with."
>
> *(Rajender, GP)*

Preventing isolation Many of the issues on which self help groups are based are often associated with being cut off from the community. Loss of mobility, mental illness, bereavement, caring for a child with a disability and diagnosis of a life-threatening condition can all have this effect. Self-helpers often talk about their extreme sense of isolation.

Self help groups offer contact with people in the same situation, some even providing a form of new community, others a social life or a stepping stone back to involvement in the wider community. It is important to recognise the issue of isolation and ways in which a professional can offer options for dealing with it. If they do not, this might be seen as poor professional practice.

> "It may be that by not offering the option of a self help group, we are condemn-
> ing that person to unnecessary isolation."   *(Peter, Social Worker)*

Questions arise around this whole question of prevention: could passing on patients and clients be a form of dumping or rejection? Can money and time really be saved? Can it be proved that it was the group that prevented a hospital re-admission? These are valid questions. Getting definitive answers to them may well be difficult. Professionals with many years' experience of working with self help groups however, able to see change over a long time span and with a variety of individuals, nonetheless speak convincingly of the value of groups as a strategy for prevention.

Improving quality

Professionals aim to provide a high quality service and professionally set standards and training, both pre-qualification and post-qualification training are some ways by which this can be achieved. Self help groups also offer a way to attain a quality service and improve professional knowledge of the issue on which the group is based.

A social work lecturer, in discussing the question of importing learning to the social work setting, sees a self help group as a source of experience from which the social worker can learn. Adams suggests that social workers should take comments from self help groups on board as part of ongoing evaluation of professional work, despite its difficulties.

> "Social workers [may feel] discomfort from the conflict between their own per-
> spective and that of the self-helpers. Yet . . . creative conflict can contribute to
> personal and professional growth."   *(Adams 1990)*

Such dilemmas and difficulties again need to be raised. How challenging is it for trained professionals to be criticised in effect by users of their services and their carers? Is telling professionals what they should be doing a function of a self help group? Good professional practice can nonetheless include getting feedback, and being educated by self help groups and this could be part of the reasons for working with them. Chapter 10 explores this topic in more depth.

Changing strategies

Linked with improving individual professional practice is the question of strategic and policy change in health and social care. A professional at field level may not be directly involved in developing policy, but they have a contribution to make by fostering and encouraging people's potential. The bigger the pool of confident self-helpers, the more likely it will be that some members of groups will come to influence services. Professionals strongly motivated to see more user involvement in planning services can increase the likelihood of this happening through their support and development role to self help groups generally.

An effective form of helping

Little formal research has been done in this country on whether belonging to a specific self help group is generally beneficial, though one study of groups for parents of children with special needs was undertaken in 1985. It concluded that overall members expressed a high level of satisfaction, both with the activities provided and the benefits they feel they have gained from belonging *(Hatch and Hinton 1986)*. A more recent report outlines ways in which self help groups can provide a variety of benefits *(Wann 1995)*, findings confirmed by my own recent research *(Wilson 1995)*. Experience of self help development workers, both nationally and locally, supports the finding that for many members self help groups are very effective. Their increasing numbers too suggest that people taking part do benefit, for people would not continue to attend and form groups if they provided no support.

Two other research studies undertaken in other countries, one in the United States, one in Germany, conclude that membership is beneficial. Compared to professionally treated alcoholics, members of Alcoholics Anonymous for example, seem to achieve abstinence at a higher rate *(Emrick 1987)*. A study of over 200 members of disease-related groups in Hamburg reported that members achieved considerable positive changes in their lives *(Trojan 1989)*. Set against this evidence must be the question of risks. An American writer, himself a self help group member as well as a researcher explores the question of 'dangers' in self help groups and sets it in context.

"Certainly self help groups are dangerous if they humiliate or depress members; if they create unthinking conformity to others' styles; if they inappropriately give vent to neurotic rage; if they unwisely escalate parents' fears and fantasies; and if, without cause, they unravel the fragile thread of hope and trust that parents have for their children's physician. However, there is no evidence in the literature that such dangers are real and commonplace. Moreover, there is no evidence that these or other dangers are more likely to occur in an autonomous or lay-led self help group than in a professionally run or supervised support group. There are some real dangers in all forms of medical and social support, whether conducted on a voluntary or statutory basis, by professionals or lay persons."   *(Chesler 1990)*

Part of weighing up reasons for working with self help groups must be the question of benefits and risks. The risk, however, is not just for the individual person who might join, there may also be risks for the professional concerned. The final topic in this chapter is related to this, for it could be that some professionals may seek involvement in self help groups to minimise risks for themselves by having some control.

For reasons of self interest

The experience of people in a small minority of self help groups is that some professionals become involved with them in order to exert control on the group or individuals within it. Anyone undertaking a detailed study of professionals and self help groups would need to give the whole question of professional power in-depth attention.

Professionals might become involved for a number of reasons, all of which come under a broad umbrella of self-interest, rather than simply power:

- To benefit from working with people helping themselves
- To get groups to fit into professional priorities
- To gain credit and status from the success of groups
- To exercise benevolent leadership
- To ensure people comply with treatment

To benefit from contact with self-helpers

Self interest is not necessarily about power. Some professionals choose to work with self help groups because of the opportunity it gives to be with people who are taking some of the responsibility for coping with a situation themselves. For some this can mean a change of role.

"You take off the professional hat and become yourself for a while. It's refreshing and personally fulfilling." *(Jane, Social Worker)*

To get groups to fit in

The experience of a small number of self help groups is that professionals wanting to work with them make assumptions that the group should fit into professional priorities and services. A member-run self help group, however, sets its own agenda and its decisions on what it does may or may not fit into professional priorities. Professionals attempting to influence a group may have misunderstood the nature of the group. A cancer group had had to face some pressures from a doctor.

"I belonged to a group for women suffering from breast cancer, which was strongly supported by the consultant. After a time it became clear that his reasons for helping us included wanting the group to fundraise for his research. He put a lot of pressure on us. We really appreciated his help as a doctor – he'd probably saved our lives – but we were more interested in giving each other support." *(Marion, Cancer Support Group)*

To gain credit

Many professionals are familiar with having to stay in the background, to hold back on claiming credit for achievement by individual users of their services. Acceptance of this may well stand them in good stead when working with self help groups. Groups are unhappy when people do attempt to claim the credit and one had had a bad experience of this.

"A lot of people try and make the public feel that they are being helpful. If it's a presentation, they want to be in the photograph, so that they look like they're the ones that are helping." *(Chris, Visually Impaired Group)*

To exercise benevolent leadership

Like the wish to claim credit, there is only occasional evidence of professionals taking the lead from a wish to be helpful from a traditional, benevolent stance, but it can happen. This could well have been the reason underlying the help given to a group based on a health centre, where a group of parents of children with disabilities had at times been led in effect by a practice nurse.

"She's been wonderful to us – and the group would never have started without her hard work. But now she is so proud of us and we daren't stop! We're a bit worried because she's retiring next year and if I'm honest, the group has tended to rely on her – and I suspect that is how she wants it."   *(Fay, Parents Group)*

To ensure people comply with treatment

A further complex issue is that of compliance. It again only happens infrequently, but is an issue which needs to be raised: could professionals be working with self help groups in order to get people to comply with treatment? One cannot prescribe attendance at a self help group, but one woman did feel that she was being pressurised to attend.

> "At one stage he was putting an awful lot of pressure on me to go to a group. I felt so guilty because I wouldn't go – it was almost as if he were saying to me, you don't want to get better, you're not making any effort."
>
> *(Kathy, Eating Disorder Group)*

Getting people to accept and conform to treatment is often part of a professional's daily job. A nurse regularly went to a diabetic group to see if people were following prescribed treatment. The group accepted her frequent attendance at their meetings, seeing it as quite acceptable that she wanted to know if what she was telling people was sticking. Many groups happily co-operate with professionals in such ways. A hospital social worker encouraged group members to visit the ward where people were waiting to have an amputation.

> "I've seen people refuse operations which would save their lives, until they met another amputee."   *(Lou, Social Worker)*

Professionals probably work with self help groups for a complex and interwoven set of reasons, some overt, others concealed. On the whole, groups' experience suggests that professionals do appreciate their value and see working with groups as part of good professional practice. To paint a realistic picture, however, self interest has to be considered as a further possible reason for being involved.

Checking your interest

Readers can check their own reasons for working with self help groups. The checklist offered below brings together issues set out in this chapter and can be used for personal assessment.

Checklist 3.1   Why work with self help groups

❑   To implement current policies in health and social care
❑   A wish to help groups become more effective
❑   To increase the number of self help groups
❑   To help people feel empowered
❑   To implement an equal opportunities policy
❑   To tap potential, enabling people to develop their skills
❑   A means of giving people the chance to be helpful
❑   To give access to other forms of help
❑   Seeing groups as a way to prevent future problems
❑   A way to learn and improve the quality of professional care
❑   To contribute to users' and carers' influence on policies
❑   A means to benefit personally from contact with self-helpers
❑   To get groups to fit in to professional priorities
❑   A wish to gain credit and status
❑   To be kind and benevolent
❑   To ensure people comply with treatment

Summary

- Before working with self help groups, assess possible reasons for doing so.

- Current policies rarely include a requirement to work with self help groups but a number endorse their contribution.

- Valuing self help groups is one reason for working with them.

- Working with self help groups can be seen as part of good professional practice.

- Some professionals work with self help groups for reasons of self-interest, including a wish to exert power.

4 Values, attitudes and challenges

Professionals with experience of working with self help groups know that it is not just a question of expertise and experience. Personal values and attitudes and traditions and outlooks of organisations and professions are both likely to be strong influences. In this chapter, the sources of personal values are first considered and the question of whether there is a need to rethink one's position is raised.

The main aim of this chapter is not so much to give a theoretical approach to this issue, but rather to offer some views of members of self help groups in order to enable professional readers to see self-helpers' perspectives. Their views are followed by an outline of the idea of two different worlds and by a summary of some of the challenges that may present themselves to professionals working with self help groups. The chapter ends by drawing some threads together, suggesting some broad principles that could be considered.

Identifying and reviewing

Wide-ranging questions of power and professionalism relevant to this issue really need in-depth discussion, but some of the many influences that underlie personal and professional values can be raised, if not explored in full. The influences on values most relevant to working with self help groups are:

- Personal experiences: health, caring responsibilities and relationships
- Gender, race and ethnic background
- Social class
- Religious and political beliefs
- Type of training undertaken, and how recently or long ago
- Past and present jobs, and reasons for choosing them
- Voluntary and community work
- The employing organisation and colleagues
- The political context of professional work

A social worker with long experience of working with self help groups reflected on this issue of influences and values.

"My belief in the importance of people doing things for themselves led me first to take posts in community development. As a result, I think I have strongly ingrained values which mean I value self help groups. But there is more to it than my personal opinions and experiences. I think we're influenced by various issues. In my experience, the broad policy of the local authority we work for can influence what we do at field level. The ethos of social work and the norms of the agency we work in – they're important too."

(Murray, Social Work Manager)

Professionals considering the source of their values and the range of influences on their work will identify conflicts between some of them and it may not be easy to recognise which are strongest. When assessing influences, some values, important in a professional setting, may be seen as less appropriate when co-operating with the self help world and may even be counterproductive. For beliefs acquired through training, endorsed by colleagues and tied to a position as a professional may not be the ones that help professionals work comfortably with self help groups.

When thinking how to start working with self help groups, consider reassessing beliefs. A lecturer in health visiting suggests the need in her field for re-appraisal.

"To become successfully involved in groups many health visitors will have to rethink their own position. They will have to consider moving away from more traditional ideas, for example, that the health professional has all the knowledge which must not be questioned, and that the health visitor's role in promoting health means lecturing people who passively accept her expertise."   *(Drennan 1988)*

The suggestion here, the need to rethink, is an issue which may well apply to many professions in a variety of settings. It is not a matter which only concerns self help groups, but rather can be seen as an appropriate way of responding to a whole social movement of consumerism in health care *(Williamson 1992)*.

The self-helpers' perspective

My own study revealed that people in self help groups can be very perceptive about attitudes professionals have towards them *(Wilson 1995)*. From experience of being on the receiving end of professional care, members were very aware of attitudes and the way these affect practice, for good and for bad. Both positive and some less helpful experiences can be grouped into three categories:

- Attitudes to individual patients and clients
- Attitudes to knowledge about an issue or illness
- Attitudes towards the value of what self help groups do

Attitudes to patients and clients

First, self-helpers saw the way they had been treated as patients and clients as being very closely linked to how their groups are perceived. Relationships were often good, and many self-helpers spoke warmly about professionals who had helped them. Martin, a member of a carers group had, though, found his GP reluctant to tell his patients about the group, or indeed anything.

"My GP, when I was trying to find out what was wrong with my wife, he wasn't very helpful at all. He was one of those who wouldn't offer anything. You had to suggest it and say – what about so-and-so."

(Martin, Alzheimer's Disease Society)

A parent of a son addicted to hard drugs saw the approach adopted by a particular organisation as influential as the individual professional. The attitude of the professionals in a drugs counselling centre, to give freedom of choice, helped the relationship between the group and the centre.

"The people that come in there are not actually told they have got to come off drugs. I think that's what makes it easier for us to work there."

(Deborah, Drugs Group)

Attitudes which seemed unhelpful to self help groups were not always attitudes to individuals or concerned with professional approaches. A member of a group for people with tinnitus, a condition which leads to sounds in the ear, identified professional attitudes to chronic illness as being a strong influence. He too had found it difficult to get professionals to publicise his group.

> "They wipe their hands when there is no cure."   *(Terry, Tinnitus Group)*

The findings of my study led to some broad conclusions about self-helpers' views about attitudes to them as individuals that they would ideally like to see:

- Members of self help groups welcome professionals who value them as individuals, "not just a number or a face"
- They appreciate professionals who encourage them in their efforts to do things for themselves
- Self-helpers want to have their needs noticed, even if there is no cure for their condition, and to be helped to make the most of life

While many professionals would also accept these points as good practice in working with individuals, self-helpers see them as closely linked to professional attitudes to self help groups.

Attitudes to knowledge

Second, members of self help groups were aware of attitudes to knowledge. An American writer with long experience of self help groups distinguishes between three types of knowledge about a condition or illness:

- Professionally gained knowledge
- Folk knowledge – common sense distilled from family or friends
- Experiential knowledge gained in a self help group

Thomasina Borkman suggests that knowledge gained from a self help group stems from the personal experience of its members and is distilled and held in the group. It becomes part of the organisation's knowledge, passed on even when the initiators of a group leave. It is different from both folk knowledge and from professional knowledge *(Borkman 1990)*. Self-helpers rarely talk about it in such terms. They know however that what they learn and share in groups is valuable, different and important.

Some self-helpers had encountered professionals who saw professionally acquired knowledge as the only route, and as some self-helpers perceived it, saw themselves as the only source of knowledge. Members of a carers group had had such experiences.

"You've sometimes got a personality problem with a doctor – I am God. I have got to be right. I cannot let the patient see that I don't know."
(Martin, Alzheimer's Disease Society)

Such attitudes were generally thought now to be less common than they were in the past and group members felt that there was less of a problem with younger doctors. The welcoming attitude of a CPN (Community Psychiatric Nurse) was more common. He was clear about why he respected the expertise he had seen in members of a tranquilliser support group.

"Members have experienced things at first hand. What they give is different and valuable in itself."
(David, CPN)

It was not only a question of valuing other people's knowledge, but of accepting limits to one's own. Professionals who accepted the limits to their knowledge were appreciated by self-helpers.

"It's not wrong, never to know it all. I think it goes back to the point that they must learn to say 'I don't know.'"
(Toni, Ileostomy Group)

Attitudes to the value of group activities

Third, self-helpers felt that what they did, the activities of the group, should be acknowledged and valued, as well as their knowledge. This had not always been the case.

"We sometimes get the impression from professional people that they see us as well meaning, but naive."
(Ellie, Carers Group)

The way help was given and taken in self help groups, the process of mutual help, may well not be the way professionals were used to. A group for people coming off tranquillisers for example, found outings a good way to start the process of accepting and giving help. This was not recognised by Social Services, who did not see what the group did was just as important as a lunch club.

"We need money for outings – somebody sits beside you on the bus and says 'I've never been out for 23 years.' Then they might get as far as the shop. There are professional people who are in this situation, in the tranquilliser trap, but they are mostly people who have been put on these things through being poor and impoverished."
(Lucy, Tranx Group)

Lucy felt that professionals don't stop to find out what a self help group does. When they do, they understand the benefits of a group better and see the differences between help from professionals and help from self help groups more clearly. Self-helpers value it when differences between the two are perceived and respected, and see efforts professionals make to find out about groups as evidence of being valued.

When relationships were going well, attitudes were rarely perceived as an issue and the study revealed many positive, helpful attitudes which self-helpers felt contributed to good working relationships. Difficulties outlined here are not the norm but rather illustrations of what can lie beneath relationships and to enable professionals to see that there may be a legacy of past encounters which self–helpers still remember.

A bridge between two worlds

Being realistic, professionals and self help groups live and work in two different worlds. It is easy for both however to make assumptions that their worlds are much the same and that it is straightforward to work in co-operation. Certain specific differences, structure, knowledge and time for example, illustrate how the two worlds differ.

Structure   Formally structured organisations are likely to find it tricky working with informally run groups. Groups may find it daunting to work with bureaucracies.

Source of knowledge   Knowledge gained through experience and in a self help group may conflict with learnt professional knowledge.

Time   Group members working on a voluntary basis have conflicting demands on their free time, while professionals are paid to do a job. Groups are largely available in the evening, professionals in the day.

The two worlds are not necessarily far apart and may even coincide and overlap, for professionals are sometimes themselves self-helpers, and professional organisations may share some of the characteristics of self help groups. But even with some similarities, groups and professionals may prefer, and need, clear separation. Professionals working with self help groups should be able to recognise, and use, bridges between them, one bridge being able to identify and build on common values. Where group members and professionals share similar values, working co-operatively becomes very much easier and is more effective.

Challenges

Co-operation in itself is not always easy, and difficulties in working together are not just the preserve of self help groups and professionals.

> "Never mind self help groups! It's often hard enough to get professionals to work inter-professionally."   *(Murray, Social Work Manager)*

While Chapter 12 will look in detail at dilemmas and difficulties likely to be encountered, some challenges relating to how people feel in a situation are raised here. Working with self help groups may be particularly challenging for a number of reasons:

- Professionals experiencing an unfamiliar situation
- Professional power and status being questioned
- A need to rethink points of view acquired over many years.

An unfamiliar experience

Professionals who venture into the self help world may be playing an unfamiliar role, and may not necessarily have the skills to deal with a situation. An example comes from a mental health team who despite long experience of co-operating with self help groups, still found it difficult. A CPN had been invited by a group to give them a talk.

> "They were a group and I was alone. They felt much stronger. I felt that I really had to be on my toes – it was really different from the usual day to day interaction with individuals."   *(Roy, CPN)*

A specialist team for visual impairment had become involved in supporting a number of new groups, a new way of working and had found it horribly difficult.

> "It's very difficult for me not to dominate."   *(Catherine, Rehabilitation Assistant)*

A challenge to power

The underlying issue of power may be more important than a new situation or lack of skills. Training, tradition and authority all combine to make the professional world very powerful. Any professional can feel their base is being undermined but the medical profession in particular is perceived by self-helpers as especially powerful, and as wanting to hold on to that power. Sometimes a position is held and endorsed by law: social workers, for example, are authorised to take children into care. Whatever the basis of power, it undoubtedly has an effect on relationships.

Members of self help groups, trying to identify reasons why some people co-operated less with them than others, speculated on whether professionals did feel threatened by group members knowing more, in a way, than they did. Or could anxiety about jobs be a reason, as a member wondered?

> "Now the group has started up, do they think we're doing their job?"
>
> *(Michael, Mental Health Group)*

A need to unlearn

Last, professionals who want to work with self help groups may well have to take some unlearning on board as part of adapting to a new way of working. In-service training provided an opportunity for one.

> "The course I went on on working with groups changed my life. I was so grateful to everyone who contributed – I've seen my job through new eyes ever since."
>
> *(Harjit, Health Visitor)*

For most people, relearning is likely to be a gradual process, influenced by contact and interaction with group members. Professionals who have experienced this, while indeed finding it challenging, find it in the long run an enriching process, benefiting both their personal and working lives.

Broad principles

I finish this chapter by suggesting some broad principles to use as a basis for working with self help groups.

Checklist 4.1 Principles for working with self help groups

❑ Acceptance of people as individuals, with strengths and limits

❑ Belief that people have the capacity to be involved with their own problem solving and care, and to develop and change

❑ Recognition of the potential ability people have to help others in the same situation and to grow in competence and skills

❑ Seeing people as part of a family, and as a member of communities, with a variety of cultural values

❑ Valuing variety and differences in approaches and methods between groups

❑ Acknowledgment of the limits to professional knowledge

❑ Recognition of the worth of knowledge gained through experience

❑ Valuing the unique contribution of self help groups as different from professional care

❑ Respect for the autonomy and integrity of a group

❑ Acceptance that some matters in a group are private and confidential

❑ Valuing assessment of what one does and, if necessary, changing it, as part of good practice

Summary

- Personal values acquired from many sources influence attitudes to self help groups and may need rethinking.

- Self-helpers link the way they are dealt with as individuals with how they are perceived as groups. They want both group knowledge and group activities to be valued.

- The two worlds of self help groups and professionals can be bridged by common values.

- Interaction between the two can be a challenging, uncomfortable process but enriching in the long term.

- A set of broad principles should be considered as a basis for work with self help groups.

5   Learning more

To work effectively with self help groups means having a reasonable degree of knowledge and information about them. Members of groups see professionals who make an effort to find out about their activities as taking them seriously and valuing their contribution.

People reading this book are likely to know a certain amount already about what groups exist, how they can be contacted and what they do. Many experienced professionals will be well informed. In this chapter, I aim to set out how both knowledge and information feed into good practice and to distinguish between the two. Four different ways of learning more are explored: using information points; visits; invitations to groups, and reading. Finally, ways of keeping up to date are suggested.

Knowledge and information

A number of factors are likely to influence professionals as they work with self help groups. Values and attitudes, explored in Chapter 4, form one type; knowledge and information also influence good practice.

Knowledge

Knowledge includes broad themes, information is more about hard details. Knowledge involves being aware of how groups work, knowing what makes them different from other forms of voluntary organisation and having the feel of particular groups. Being knowledgeable means knowing about the benefits of belonging, but professionals setting out to increase their knowledge should also aim to become better informed about the limits of groups. They should become aware, as most groups are themselves, of the boundaries within which they work and the limits to what they can offer. Becoming knowledgeable about groups avoids having to draw on myths and hearsay.

The checklist below suggests some of the questions that a knowledgeable, experienced professional might be able to answer.

Checklist 5.1   Topics a knowledgeable professional might expect to know about

❑   What are the essential ingredients of a self help group?
❑   Are all groups much the same?
❑   Are branches of a national organisation alike in different areas?
❑   What range of activities might be undertaken?
❑   Do they all have regular meetings? How often? Day or evening?
❑   How are groups formed?
❑   Are they social groups?
❑   Are they open to newcomers or closed?
❑   Do members have to pay to join?
❑   What places are used for meetings?

Information

Information, overlapping with knowledge, includes knowing what groups exist, how to get in touch with them and where and when they meet. Being well informed about self help groups may not mean holding all this detail directly, for this may be impractical, and because so many groups change, it may even be an inefficient way to go about it. More important than holding a list of a large number of groups is having an awareness that there might be a group for a certain condition or issue, and then knowing where to go to find out details.

Variation

Just how knowledgeable and how well informed a professional needs to be will depend on their job. There will inevitably be variation, depending in part on where they are working. Working in a community team is likely to require different information, for example, from a specialist ward in a hospital. Nor will all professionals need to know about all groups. Working in a particular area, mental health or visual impairment say, may mean that knowing about groups concerned with those issues should be part of a knowledge base, but that it is not necessary to have wide knowledge of other groups.

There are not always clearcut boundaries to what information and knowledge will be needed. A physical condition or disability may sometimes lead to mental health problems. There are some broadly-based self help groups which set out to meet the needs of a range of people. Family members may have special needs. Developing knowledge about groups needs some assessment of whether it should cover a wide range of groups or a specialist area. Drawing boundaries too closely may, though, be inappropriate.

A conscious effort

For two reasons, it may well be necessary to make a conscious effort to learn more about self help groups. The first is the limits to the groups themselves and the second variation in professional resources and traditions.

Limits to groups

In an ideal world, groups should tell professionals they exist. Some make it easy for professionals to learn about what they do and how they can be contacted. They may have become quite experienced in publicity and public relations. Groups in this first category are probably well established, may be local branches of a national organisation, have reasonable resources and have found their way round professional communication networks. In this case, it may not be necessary to have to work hard to learn about them.

It is more likely that groups have neither the resources, nor the knowledge and experience that might be needed. Nor are they always able to be consistent. A member may promote the group energetically, but then may leave. A member's personal life may suddenly change, meaning they are not able to do as much as they would like to do. It is best to expect to have to make a conscious effort to learn about groups in this second category, rather than count on them informing you.

Differing professional resources

Some professions make it part of the way they work to find out about resources and organisations in their area. Health visitor students for example, undertake a community profile as part of their professional practice. It is seen as crucial.

"Information gathered from informal and formal sources to provide a picture of a community is the key to health visiting, whether with individuals or with groups." *(Drennan 1988)*.

If a profession or workbase has traditions of developing and holding a wide knowledge base of community activity, it will be reasonably easy to become informed about self help groups. It may help to visualise a continuum, with different emphases. Working in an agency at the lower end of the spectrum is likely to mean more individual effort has to be made.

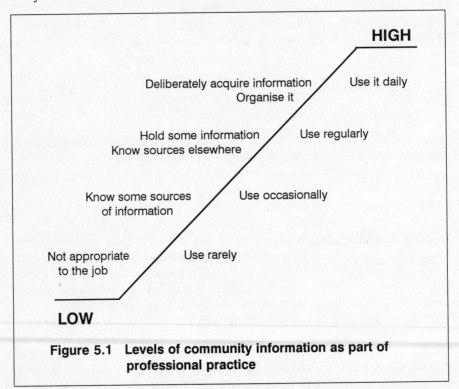

HIGH

Deliberately acquire information   Use it daily
Organise it

Hold some information   Use regularly
Know sources elsewhere

Know some sources   Use occasionally
of information

Not appropriate   Use rarely
to the job

LOW

Figure 5.1   Levels of community information as part of professional practice

While some agencies create their own information database, it is not easy to do this without proper resources, as a Visual Impairment Team found.

> "We put it on a disc, but it was difficult because they kept changing. It became an administrative nightmare!"   *(Bet, Rehabilitation Assistant)*

How much effort is needed may depend too on how long someone has been in post. Coming new to a post may well mean having to begin to create a personal knowledge base. Working in the same area for a long time is likely to lead to knowing a great deal about community resources.

> "I have worked in this area for 16 years. You store up the knowledge over the years."   *(Angela, Health Visitor)*

At some point in the future this subject may become part of professional training. At present this only happens occasionally, meaning that learning on the job and probably having to make a conscious effort to do so is the sole way for most professionals to go about learning more.

Drawing on personal experience

There is, however, one other route. Most professionals, as individuals, will have run into some difficulties in their personal lives: health problems, bereavement, as part of being a parent, for example. They may have met discrimination and prejudice. Professional support in dealing with such situations may have been enough or help from family, friends, neighbours, a local organisation, church or other religious centre may also have helped. In addition to these, help from people who had gone through the same situation may have been just what people felt they needed.

> "When my father died I found myself turning particularly to friends who had also lost a parent. Everyone was very kind, but others who had gone through it too seemed to be able to say just the right thing and not to mind when I told my story yet again."
> *(Jean, Community Worker)*

> "We meet for lunch every now again, it's an informal group for black women managers. It's a place to be myself and to hear how other people have coped with double discrimination."
> *(Lois, Social Services Manager)*

Part of a professional knowledge base about self help groups may lie in personal experience of mutual help, even if it did not involve joining a group. Thinking further about it may help to understand more of the process of mutual help in a self help group. If this has been your experience, then you are likely to have come to value being with people in the same situation, for whom explanations are not needed. You will have felt encouraged by the model some offer, giving evidence that there is light at the end of the tunnel. Help won't have been by appointment, but when needed. It is likely that you will also have experienced some of the limits to mutual help.

Not all people reading this book will have had these experiences, nor is it an essential requirement to have done so in order to work successfully with self help groups. But for some, recalling past personal experiences may help build up a knowledge base. Professionals who have themselves been or are members of a self help group will naturally draw on their experience of being a member.

How to learn more

Professionals will come with varying amounts of experience and resources on which to draw. To increase a level of knowledge and information a number of methods can be used: using information points; undertaking visits to groups; inviting groups to a professional meeting; and reading.

Information points

In an average medium-sized town there are likely to be upwards of a hundred self help groups. It is not practical for the average professional to know all that exist, nor is it necessarily a good use of time to build up a personal database. Rather, it may be better to identify sources of information about groups and know and use them. A variety of possible local sources of information may exist, summarised in Checklist 5.2.

Checklist 5.2   Local information points

❑ Self help groups project
❑ Council for Voluntary Service
❑ Library
❑ Citizens Advice Bureau
❑ Local newspapers and radio
❑ Local directories
❑ Community Health Council
❑ Local authority information centre
❑ Hospital database
❑ Health information service/healthline
❑ Social Services Department

Some of these at least will be accessible and useful to most professionals. Keeping a note of relevant telephone numbers and opening hours, and making sure of having current copies of any publications will mean being able to get access to them as needed. In areas where there is a specialist self help groups worker, often attached to a local Council for Voluntary Service, it is likely that there will be a computerised database of groups and a regularly updated directory. Use them as a first place of call.

Regional and national sources of information may also be useful, and in the case of rare conditions, may be the only way to get details. Checklist 5.3 includes some suggestions.

Checklist 5.3 Regional and national information points

❑ Regional Healthline
❑ In Touch
❑ National Council for Voluntary Organisations
❑ College of Health
❑ National organisations e.g. Cancerlink, BACUP
❑ Patients Association

It may also be possible to go directly to groups. Well established groups produce literature about their work and may be willing to send it in the post, though some may ask an enquirer to send a stamped addressed envelope. Others raise funds by selling literature, and it may be necessary to order and pay for their material.

Visiting groups

Visiting groups can be one very useful way of finding out more about them. Some groups welcome this.

> "I get student psychologists, student nurses that come and sit in on the group for an afternoon and that is good." *(Dora, Tranx Group)*

Others feel used too much by students doing a project but welcome visitors for themselves.

> "They will ring up and say I am doing a project, can I come along and meet some of the carers. We will say yes, but I think to myself that it would be nice if they just rang up and asked without a project or a paper to do."
> *(Ellie, Alzheimer's Disease Group)*

It is important to assess whether a visit is possible or not for one cannot assume that attending a group meeting is always appropriate. Groups are set up to meet the needs of members, not as a way of educating professionals, and it may be intrusive for any outsider to attend.

> "The meetings are for carers only. We keep the professionals out. It's for us to talk." *(Matt, Carers Group)*

There are pros and cons to professionals sitting in on a group meeting (Chapter 10, page 116) and any visitor needs to be conscious of their role

(Chapter 8, page 92), Visiting a group requires sensitivity and needs careful thought. Groups are entitled to say that they would prefer no visitors, and any request to attend should be phrased in such a way that they can say this.

One method of visiting groups that does work is attending open meetings. AA (Alcoholics Anonymous), an important group for anyone wanting to learn about self help groups, holds regular open meetings. These will be a normal AA meeting but members will know that there may be visitors there and will welcome their attendance. Other groups put on special open events. Groups which have outside speakers will normally welcome outsiders at their meetings too, and these, while not normally described as open meetings, may well be open to visitors.

Not all groups are large enough or sufficiently well established to organise open meetings, nor may they have speakers but they may be willing to allow a visitor to sit in on a meeting. It is essential to ask beforehand if this is possible, and these guidelines on visiting groups should be followed.

Checklist 5.4   Guidelines for visiting groups

- ❑ Do not assume a visit is possible
- ❑ See yourself as a visitor
- ❑ Ask permission well beforehand, unless it is advertised as an open meeting
- ❑ Be aware that the person approached may need to check with other members of the group before agreeing
- ❑ Allow plenty of time for you to get in touch and then for the group contact to ask other members for their agreement
- ❑ Accept any refusal to attend with understanding
- ❑ Go alone, or with only one colleague
- ❑ Do not intrude on the process and business of the group
- ❑ Be prepared to have to stay silent for the whole meeting
- ❑ Understand that what is said may well be confidential
- ❑ Write and thank the group after the visit
- ❑ Feed back your experience to colleagues, within the boundaries of confidentiality

---

Inviting groups

An alternative way of learning about groups is to extend them an invitation to visit you. There may well be meetings already arranged that could be used for this and which would mean an audience was guaranteed.

"There is a unit meeting once a month. You could have a session at the end, half an hour even. You could learn a lot that way." *(Deirdre, Health Visitor)*

Groups normally welcome such invitations, seeing them as giving an opportunity to publicise what they do; some though may just not have enough members with time in the day to take it on. If they have people free, it is likely that while some members will take this on with ease, others may find it a taxing experience. Some guidelines again may help make the visit a success for everyone.

Checklist 5.5 Guidelines for inviting groups to give talks

- ❑ Make contact directly first, by phone or by seeing a member
- ❑ Give good notice and offer a choice of dates
- ❑ Suggest that people come in pairs if they want, one to speak and one to support and help answer questions
- ❑ Agree the length of the talk and the length of time for questions
- ❑ Agree the topic, eg how the group works, or the issue it covers, or both
- ❑ Say why you are inviting them and who will be attending
- ❑ Ask if people have any particular needs, e.g. accessible room
- ❑ Offer to pay travel costs, and any caring costs if you can
- ❑ Ask groups to bring literature with them
- ❑ Send a map, with parking marked, when confirming the arrangement in writing
- ❑ If agreed long in advance, reconfirm arrangements near the time by phone
- ❑ Alert reception staff that group members are expected
- ❑ Make introductions, of both speakers and audience
- ❑ Agree any appropriate groundrules on confidentiality, e.g. first names only
- ❑ Clarify what questions speakers feel able to deal with
- ❑ Feel you can gently keep the speaker to the agreed time, but remember they may be doing this for the first time
- ❑ Pay expenses in cash on the day if possible
- ❑ Write and thank the speaker for coming

Reading

A final way to develop knowledge about groups is to read about them. This may need some perseverance. One cannot assume that one can just go to the local library and find what is wanted on the shelves. There may be resources within an agency to help: a health promotion resource centre, a social services library or a postgraduate education centre. Such centres may help in getting books and articles or by undertaking a literature search.

National organisations publish newsletters and booklets. For professionals with a specialist interest in a certain area, getting on a national organisation's mailing list or subscribing to a newsletter may be useful. If enough staff in an agency are interested, the organisation might take out a subscription. Well established local self help groups will sometimes put a professional agency on their mailing list. Some groups find this very helpful to them.

> "I think you need to let professionals know what you are up to. We had a session of pruning the newsletter distribution list and then we got phone calls saying we do want it, we do find it valuable."   *(Kay, Twins Group)*

A few guidelines on this too may help, summarised in Checklist 5.6.

Checklist 5.6   Guidelines for being on groups' mailing lists

- ❑ Ask for one copy of a newsletter first to see if it would be useful
- ❑ Ask if there is a subscription arrangement
- ❑ Check if a contribution to postage would be a help
- ❑ Pass copies round colleagues
- ❑ Inform the group of any changes of name or address

Keeping up to date

Like any area of professional practice, being well informed also means keeping up to date.

A changing scene

In any one year, about half the self help groups in an area will probably change in some way. Some come to an end; new groups will start; contact people, meeting places and days will change. Groups may change in character and activities.

Using methods suggested in this chapter will mean keeping up to date happens to some extent. Close contact with a small number of groups, relevant to a specialist area of work, will mean being kept informed quite naturally. Professionals working in an area where there is a self help project will find it easier too. Others may need to make more of a conscious effort, using students, or sharing knowledge and information with colleagues.

Students on placement may be a useful resource, for it might be appropriate for them to undertake a project to check and update information held in an agency. While being useful to the organisation, this would also be a good means of developing their knowledge.

Sharing information with colleagues is a useful method of increasing knowledge in this field. It may be possible to use team meetings or internal news-sheets to pass information on.

To conclude this chapter, there will be limits to what can be achieved alone. Effective learning may need the support and resources of colleagues, manager and an organisation. It may help to give some thought to the extent to which this learning process can be undertaken by you as an individual, and to what extent it has to be helped by the organisation. It may well be that an agency is already committed, informed and with enough resources for many of the methods outlined above to be in use already. In this case, and where there is a culture of valuing community information generally, learning more will be easier than if there is not already this degree of interest.

Pioneers in an agency or lone interested people may have to be realistic: it will be a hard job. In this case, it may help both to develop individual knowledge, but also to consider whether it would be possible to influence an agency's practice.

Summary

- Good practice in working with self help groups includes being knowledgeable and informed about them.

- Groups appreciate professionals who make a conscious effort to become so and are likely to respond positively within their limits.

- Some professionals may be able to draw on personal experience as one way of increasing their knowledge.

- Four different means of learning more can be used.

- Good practice also means keeping up to date.

Section two

Ways to work

6   Linking

Linking people with self help groups is probably the most effective way in which a professional can help a group – but not intrude upon it. The group is helped; the individual concerned is given an option; and the quality of care is extended. Almost any professional could consider building linking people with self help groups into their work.

In this chapter this important aspect of practice will be explored in detail and the crucial role that professionals can play is discussed. Principles, process and practice are looked at in depth, while some dilemmas and difficulties that are likely to be part of good practice are summed up and debated.

A crucial role

Professionals can provide a crucial link between a group and people who might like to join it. Some groups get all their members through professionals, others perhaps only five per cent, but whatever the proportion there is potentially a very important role to play. For some professionals it may already be an est-ablished part of day-to-day working practice, an automatic part of a procedure or included in a publication distributed to all people using a service.

"I always put newly diagnosed families in touch with the parents' support group." *(Katherine, Physiotherapist)*

"Information about local groups is included in the antenatal book – I'll say remember the book I gave you, have a look in there." *(Annie, Health Visitor)*

If not already part of normal practice, the first step could be to become more aware of this important key role, looking at it from three different approaches:

- Meeting an individual's needs
- Strengthening a group
- Promoting equal access

Meeting an individual's needs

A linking role can be pivotal because the individual using professional services may not know that there is a group for people in the same situation as themselves. They may not even know that self help groups exist as a possible form of help.

> "Half of them don't know what's going on."
>
> *(Kaneez, Asian Mothers and Children Group)*

Many people are likely to need to be offered information and a professional cannot assume that they will find out about self help groups in other ways. Others may know groups exist, but lack the confidence to do something about joining one, meaning their need may be to talk it through or be introduced to the group.

Strengthening a group

When professionals regularly link clients and patients with a group, it can be an extremely helpful form of support for a group, as opposed to an individual. Even when groups make big efforts to undertake publicity and advertising, they are rarely well known. To be viable, some groups may need a constant renewal of membership. Having systems by which professionals put people in touch (or the lack of them) can make or break a group.

People in some groups leave naturally after a time, either as the next step in coming to terms with their situation, or they find that the group is no longer meeting their needs. This can be a natural step for the individuals concerned, but cause difficulties for the group. Numbers can drop to the extent that unless new members join, it may end.

Giving equal access

Professionals who regularly put people in touch with groups are ensuring that all who might want to attend can do so. A professional's contribution can be a helpful way of putting an equal opportunities policy into action. Some groups are aware that their membership does not include people from all ethnic backgrounds. One member speculated about the reasons for this, wondering if the cause lay in the group, or whether people were not being told the group existed.

> "Not many black people come to our group. I've been wondering – is it us, or is it that the doctors aren't telling them that the gro1up exists?"
>
> *(Bill, Tinnitus Group)*

Many self help groups based on a single issue aim to be open to everyone who feels they would like to join, aiming to be multicultural rather than initiated for one ethnic group. Professional channels may then help groups get more of a cross-section of people attending, as a group based on lupus found. (Lupus, a form of arthritis experienced by both white and black people, affects people with dark skins disproportionately.)

> "One of the doctors doing research into lupus makes a point of telling everyone he sees about the group. It's as a result of his encouragement, I'm sure, that our group is a mix of black and white people." *(Gail, Lupus Group)*

Some people prefer groups which are based both on culture as well as on issues (an example might be an Asian diabetes group), a question discussed further in Chapter 11. A professional with access to information about a range of groups will be able to give people choice on what group they might attend.

A final point relates to discrimination. There can be a practice of exclusion operating in self help groups, perhaps unwittingly, which a professional may be able to question. It may only be through feedback to a professional that this is known and some action taken about it.

> "A social worker told me that she had put her client in touch with a group. Oh no, they said, this group is not for you, there are other groups for Asian people."
>
> *(Harminder, Self Help Worker)*

Professionals who learn that this is happening may be in a position to draw the group's attention to how people feel and to discuss with the group how this might be avoided in the future.

Principles

For all these reasons, professionals have an important part to play in giving access to self help groups. Group members in my research study felt strongly that everyone should have the chance to choose whether to go to a group or not, so that access was equal. Their experience suggests that information is rarely passed on systematically, meaning that, as one group saw it, there was an unfair screening system operating.

> "To have a screening service, well, what it means effectively is that some people get a better service than others."   *(Kathryn, Twins Group)*

Guiding principles

The practice of putting people in touch will depend on a particular work situation and the needs of the people with whom an agency is concerned, but some underlying principles are likely to apply whatever the professional setting. A checklist of principles for practice is offered:

Checklist 6.1   Principles for putting people in touch with self help groups

❏   Everyone should be told rather than a selected few

❏   People should be given the chance to make an informed choice

❏   Situations of 'dumping' people on groups should be avoided

❏   People should not have to fear they may lose the help of the professional by going, or not going to a group

❏   Confidentiality of personal information should be maintained

❏   Accurate information should be made available as far as possible

---

Selection or telling everyone

Later in this chapter some common dilemmas and difficulties are explored. This question of selection or telling everyone is one dilemma, for some professionals want to be selective, seeing good practice as matching a client with a group. Groups in the study did not by and large agree, feeling that it was not possible for professionals to perceive one person as being in greater need than another and that fine distinctions were wrong.

> "To make fine distinctions between people isn't very helpful. At that point, they may not be ready for a group, but be happy just to know it's there. We've had three years' delay before people actually come. If they didn't have that inform-ation, they could never come."   *(Phil, Mental Health Group)*

A group of parents of children with arthritis had experienced this selection with one family where the professional's judgment had turned out to be wrong.

> "There was a young boy who had only got it – the arthritis – in his knee. The physios felt it wasn't worth telling them about the group – 'it was only a knee'. Well! When I actually did get hold of the mother, she thought it was the end of the world. Her son couldn't play football and she was devastated, absolutely devastated. *(Judith, Parents of Children with Arthritis Group)*

The recommended main principle is to tell everyone that a group exists, and to give them enough information so that they can make an informed choice about whether to become a member or not.

The process of putting people in touch

Think through what is involved in the process before considering the practice of putting people in touch. There are two particular issues to consider: the question of whether it is a referral or not and how closely a professional might be involved.

Not a 'referral'

Referral is a common part of professional practice, a normal procedure accepted by clients and patients. It is usual to be referred on to other parts of professional care for other specialist services. When a professional links someone with a self help group, however, it is not a referral. Instead, it is more accurate to see it as a process of putting people in touch with a group. Checklist 6.2 summarises differences between the two processes.

Checklist 6.2   A comparison between putting people in touch and referral

	PUTTING PEOPLE IN TOUCH	REFERRAL
CHOICE	Made by individual	Made by professional
SEEN AS ESSENTIAL TREATMENT?	No	Yes
CONFIDENTIAL?	Yes – individual tells group about themselves	No – professional passes on details
DECISION ON WHEN TO JOIN	Made by individual	Made by professional

Seeing the process not as referral, but as a method of putting people in touch, acknowledges that the person concerned makes the choice of whether to go or not. It enables people to decide not to go to a group without worrying that they may incur professional disapproval. They can be confident that only information they have agreed may be given to the group has been passed on. When they join, they can choose how much and at what point they share personal information with other people. And they go to the group motivated by a personal feeling of wanting to help themselves, not just because a professional feels they should attend.

Making it clear that it is not a referral prevents confusion, for if it is presented as a referral it may be interpreted as a requirement that they should attend. Long traditions of respect for professionals, particularly doctors, by their patients and clients can lead to assumptions that everything they suggest must be followed.

How involved in the process

Think about how closely involved a professional might be in the process, for it can vary from them being very uninvolved to being closely concerned. It is not simply 'good' to be detached and 'bad' to be involved, or vice versa, it being again a question of what is appropriate for the situation, the group and the individual. Nor need there be necessarily only one route, for it may work best for there to be a number of interrelated ways in which people are put in touch with self help groups by professionals.

The practice of putting people in touch

Ways in which people can be put in touch can be divided into:

- Displaying information
- Passing on information on a one-to-one basis
- Introducing someone to the group

Displaying information

Noticeboards are a practical, effective and reasonably straightforward method that many professionals use. They may use a general noticeboard, one dedicated to community information or one purely for self help groups.

> "I pin up information – anything which seems relevant to the families using our service. Then people are free to make up their own minds."
>
> *(Katherine, Physiotherapist)*

There are many advantages to displaying posters and leaflets:

- People can learn about groups informally
- They can copy information without having to ask anyone
- They may get a choice of groups
- The groups know that people visiting that agency will learn that they exist

The disadvantages of posters on noticeboards are:

- It may be necessary to buy and put up extra boards
- Posters can get out of date
- A board can get used for a variety of information and be confusing
- Nobody may feel responsible for the board continuing to look attractive and informative
- It will take time and trouble to locate information

There are also sometimes issues for professionals to face. By displaying a poster is a group being endorsed? Could the presence of a poster be upsetting to some clients? The experience of some groups refused permission to put up a poster suggests that occasionally professionals do pose these questions.

"GP's don't like our posters because it upsets the ante-natal mums – which you can understand in a way, but there again, these things have to be faced."

(Jo, Downs Syndrome Group)

"The doctor refused to put up our poster. He said we would learn bad habits from each other."   *(Kathy, Women's Eating Disorders Group)*

Generally however, noticeboards are an effective, indirect way of putting people in touch with groups. Most professional organisations could adopt this method with relatively little effort or expense. But keeping boards attractive and up to date requires commitment by management as well as by individual workers, systems, money and staff time.

Passing on information on a one-to-one basis

A more direct method is to offer or give someone information on a one-to-one basis. The questions of when and how someone might be put in touch with a group need considered depending on how often a professional is likely to see them: different approaches may be suitable depending on whether there is ongoing contact or a brief encounter. A number of issues need to be thought through:

- Taking advantage of key opportunities
- Using the opportunity of ongoing contact
- Giving people the chance to weigh up the pros and cons
- Providing written information

Key opportunities   There can be crucial opportunities, which if missed, may mean either someone never gets to hear about the group, or may do so much later than they would have liked. Hospital discharge can be one of the key opportunities to put people in touch with a group.

"The Sister at the A & E Department gave us a card. I phoned as soon as I got home. I sat on the stairs and talked for an hour. Not everyone wants that immediate link – but it was what I needed when my baby died."

(Angela, Cot Deaths Group)

"My husband had been home a few weeks when he found a leaflet in his jacket pocket. That nurse gave it to me when I was discharged, he said, she thought I might find it useful. I think I'll go next week."

(Jenny, Cardiac Support Group)

Linking people with a group as part of the process of hospital discharge has been recommended by an Audit Commission report (1993). Hospitals find it practicable and patients, families and groups alike welcome the practice.

The principle of seizing key opportunities can be put into practice in a number of ways, not necessarily only on discharge. A Drugs Centre uses the initial phone enquiry for example.

> "If a friend or family member rings them up, they are automatically given our number – it doesn't matter if the person on the phone thinks they need that help or not – they will say, there is a support group, here's the number. But you can still come in here if you want." *(Deborah, Parents Drugs Group)*

Ongoing contact Seeing someone as a regular client gives the chance to think of the best time to mention a group and the chance to touch on it more than once. It may be work well to raise attending as a possibility early on and return to the subject later.

> "I'll tell them that there is a group – come back to me for more details if you're interested." *(Pat, Health Visitor)*

Groups suggest that people need to know that a group exists sooner rather than later. A twins group for example found that many new parents only got to know about the group after the babies' arrival. Most people would have liked contact and support before the babies were born as well.

Accepting that someone may well choose not to go to a group is part of the process. It can be quite common, particularly among older people, but should not stop groups being mentioned. In discussing it, spell out that the group is not being 'prescribed', nor do they have to stop receiving professional care if they join. One woman assumed she had to go when the health visitor mentioned it.

> "I discovered that one of my clients felt she had to go to the group, because I'd suggested it. If she didn't, she feared I might stop visiting her. I was horrified –
> - I hadn't intended to give that impression at all. Luckily the group rang me up and we sorted it out." *(Bev, Specialist Health Visitor)*

Weighing up pros and cons Professional workers may be helpful, not only in giving or offering the information, but in supporting someone in weighing up whether to go or not, and when might be the best time for them. A Health Visitor regularly discusses pros and cons of groups, feeling it can be an essential part of the process if the person concerned has a debilitating illness like Multiple Sclerosis. Meeting people who are worse than they are may not be easy.

"I'll suggest they write for written information first. I'll discuss the difficulties they may face."   *(Pat, Health Visitor)*

The initiative for discussion may come from the potential member and even if the group is not known to the professional, talking it over may be very useful.

"A parent had written for details of a support group she'd seen mentioned in a women's magazine. She used me as a sounding board to help her decide whether to go or not."   *(Katherine, Physiotherapist)*

In areas where there are large numbers of groups, there may be a choice between groups, giving a professional the opportunity to help someone weigh up which group is best for them. An advantage of this is that the potential problem of being seen to endorse one particular group is avoided. In practice, however, unless someone is willing and able to travel, there is unlikely to be much choice.

Providing written information   Putting someone in touch with a group may well require more than telling them about it or discussing the pros and cons of membership. It may also be necessary to give them some written information. It may be possible to acquire a selection of literature, as suggested in the previous chapter, remembering there is a risk of handing out out-of-date literature – it is important to check.

"They still have the old leaflets despite the fact I sent the midwives new ones with the new number on. So they call the old number. She tells them the new number to phone. By that time you may lose them."   *(Kathryn, Twins Group)*

There are alternatives to leaflets: in areas where there is a self help project or an active Council for Voluntary Service (CVS), it may be possible to use a directory of self help groups and simply copy the relevant entry. If there has been a press report about a group, a press cutting can be photocopied. Having something written to keep can be very important.

"I put the press cutting behind the clock. It stayed there for months till I plucked up my courage and phoned the group. It was the best thing I ever did."   *(Vera, Alzheimer's Disease Society)*

As long as the person concerned is happy for their name and address to be handed on, a local self help project or the group itself may be able to send some literature direct.

"The Sister will phone up and say, I've got a couple here, one suffering from Alzheimer's. I send all the meeting dates and any literature they want."

(Ellie, Alzheimer's Disease Society)

The challenge is to get the right balance between doing too much for the potential member and facilitating the process of getting information. People in distress, often shocked by a diagnosis, appreciate it when someone takes the initiative and gets some written information for them.

Introducing someone to the group

A familiar professional may be the best person to ease the process by making arrangements for a new member to meet members before they actually join, or occasionally it may be appropriate, with permission from the group, to go with the person to their first meeting – after all, walking into a room full of strangers alone is not always easy.

"I've walked into a group with someone and actually sat there with them at first, because that's what they've asked for."   *(Ray, CPN)*

"If they have a new family come for physiotherapy, they will say – do you want Judith to contact you, or do you want to contact her? It's a lot easier for them if I make the first move."   *(Judith, Arthritis Parents Group)*

Centres of various sorts – day centres, mental health centres, family centres and so on – may be well placed to invite groups to make visits. Hospitals have special opportunities which they can take to help this process of introduction.

"We go along to the rehabilitation every week, and mash the tea for them. Every six weeks we do a talk about the group to the people on the course."

(Keith, Cardiac Support Group)

"We're very, very welcome on the ward. We get phone calls saying, can you come, there is someone who wants to talk. And at least one of our members goes to physiotherapy every week."   *(Cheryl, Amputees Group)*

While this can be ideal, meeting members beforehand may not always be possible with a small voluntary group. Nor may group members feel that it is the best approach, as a Probation Officer found:

"A young man I was working with was very nervous about the prospect of going alone to the group, though he really wanted to. At last I managed to get them on the phone. But they said, no, he had to come along by himself, they had all had to and it was part of the process of joining."   ,   *(Gay, Probation Officer)*

Through experience, and through feedback from people once they have gone, the right method in any one situation can emerge. The principle to take on board is that introductions may be very helpful – and a professional may be the only person to make them.

Ask for feedback

A final point is getting feedback: if you can, ask people how they got on. Occasionally this may be seen as an inroad into an activity which the person involved sees as their own concern, but if the question is phrased suitably it need not be seen as intrusive. It is acceptable to ask this in order to become better informed about the group, and so be able to give other people a better idea about what is involved in joining. Good practice for self help groups includes advice that group members should not wait to be asked, they should tell professionals how they got on *(Wilson 1994a)*. But this may not always happen – it may be necessary for the professional to take the initiative.

Feedback can also be a way of checking up on the best way to make the link. For example, people might have preferred to have met group members beforehand, rather than go cold to a group; or they might have welcomed written information. Unless one asks, what seems to work best may not become known.

Dilemmas and difficulties

Part of good practice for professionals in working with self help groups is recognising problems and accepting that these may be inevitable. Even this seemingly non-intrusive, straightforward practice of putting people in touch brings dilemmas and difficulties. These may be divided into five categories:

- Two different worlds have different outlooks
- The dilemma of endorsement
- Commitment to clients, wanting the best for them
- The difficulty of accepting a label
- The risk of leaving people isolated

Two worlds, two outlooks

Group members who strongly value knowledge gained through experience want other people to have the opportunity of access to the wealth of knowledge in their groups. The issue of the different routes to knowledge in the two worlds of self help groups and professionals was touched on in Chapter 2. Group members are likely to feel that people should automatically be put in touch with their groups.

Their view may well conflict with the professional perspective, which may stress the need to be selective. The professional may feel they should choose which groups are mentioned or publicised, and which clients or patients should be linked with them.

The dilemma of endorsement

The question of whether a group is being recommended by displaying a poster or mentioning it can be a very real dilemma for some professionals. Others see the issue as one of making information available and, if needed, helping someone to make up their own mind, perceiving the process not as a referral, but rather as linking people with common interests and problems.

There can however be some deep concerns. Some groups, though probably only a very few, can be dogmatic and follow a cause which a professional may not feel able to support. A small number, probably more correctly seen as campaigning groups, may urge opposition to professional care or suggest suing public authorities. Others, while not campaigning vociferously for opposition, can be very critical of systems of professional care.

More common are situations where a group is not so much hostile as ineffective. Professionals may know of well-meaning groups, on the surface open to all but in practice are cliquey. Trying to change them is not always successful, though support may help. There can be a risk of setting professional standards for a lay, volunteer-run activity but it may be indeed that the group cannot offer effective support, while claiming to do so. While racist or other unacceptable behaviour would be practice that a professional would not want to condone by publicising the group, not being very effective is less clearcut.

This dilemma of endorsement needs to be faced, perhaps though more of a problem for people with traditional, controlling attitudes than for those who welcome empowerment and involvement by users and carers of services.

Commitment to clients

A further dilemma arises from commitment to people who are clients and patients, often vulnerable and for whom professional responsibility is felt.

Should a professional allow them to take risks? Do professional standards of care require selecting groups and matching clients?

Part of high standards of professional care may well mean ensuring that vulnerable people are not exposed to unnecessary risks. A feeling of security may be needed, rather than the experience of being plunged into an unknown group, exposed to everyone else's problems. Good professional practice may involve ensuring that people avoid unnecessary painful situations, at least until they are able to cope with them. Or it may be felt that the individual should be matched with the group, especially if there are a range from which to choose.

Protection can however become control, the issue here being that one may become paternalistic rather than professional. Furthermore, there may be no choice of group within reach, so matching the client to the right group may not be an option.

People concerned with a whole family, or an individual and their carer face a further dilemma – who is their client? If a client is the person with learning disabilities for example, should one put their parents in touch with a local parents' group, perhaps with a different and a more traditional approach than the professional agency? If there is no more to be done for an ill person, is there still a responsibility for relatives and carers? There may be a question of how far responsibility for putting people in touch with groups should go and perhaps, sometimes, a conflict of interest.

Accepting a label

Some self help groups cover a variety of situations. A women's health group, or a positive health group for example, allow people to join without having to define, or necessarily accept, a particular health or social need. Becoming a member of an issue-related self help group based on a particular, defined matter may well involve acceptance of having a particular problem. Particularly in the case of mental health and in illnesses where diagnosis is a lengthy process, being given and accepting the label may be a difficult challenge.

The dilemma for the professional is related but different. How best can one assess which people may want or not want to face up to a diagnosis or the reality of the situation? To what extent is mentioning a self help group helpful? What timing is best? These are real concerns.

The risk of isolation

The final point in this chapter concerns the role of self help groups in preventing or helping to deal with isolation. The experience of joining a group may be a crucial opportunity for people to see that their situation is not abnormal, the stories in Chapter 2 illustrating the way self help group membership resulted in people no longer feeling alone, and the satisfaction they gained from being helpful. By not telling people about groups, could they instead be being left in isolation by professionals, who might give access but do not?

Isolation comes through as a powerful and moving theme when people speak of their experiences before joining a self help group. Members of groups in the fields of disability, mental health, bereavement, families and chronic illness all speak consistently of how their group had helped them either deal with isolation or avoid it in the first place. Isolation is generally accepted as leading to further difficulties; mental health problems may arise from physical illness, for example and bring further demands on professionals in health and social services.

Being isolated may also mean that people are deprived of an opportunity to be helpful to others. Group members frequently stress how beneficial it is to be helpful. By not giving people the chance to grow into a helping relationship, could they be being excluded from an opportunity of self development and greater involvement in the community? Such issues need to be faced too.

Summary

- See putting people in touch with self help groups as an important part of good practice. It can be a crucial role.

- Consider adopting some underlying principles, particularly that of telling everyone rather than being selective.

- Be clear that the process of putting people in touch is not referral.

- Choose from a variety of ways in which it can be done, and see that there can be varying degrees of involvement in the process.

- Accept that dilemmas and difficulties of various kinds are an integral part of this work, to be identified and faced.

7   Starting off

This chapter looks at ways in which a professional can help a new self help group get going. In general, groups welcome appropriate support as they begin but becoming involved in a new group can be a difficult job: helping too much can put at risk the ability of members to run the group themselves; giving too little help can be interpreted by members as ignoring rather than valuing what they are doing. Doing too little can also mean that a potentially useful source of advice and support for the group is lost.

The chapter begins by posing some questions and then identifying some principles on which work can be based. Seven different roles for professionals are outlined and possible difficulties that could be experienced are summarised. The chapter ends with an outline of a possible alternative approach to the development of new self help groups, involving the creation of an environment in which they can flourish.

Questions to ask

Helping a new self help group to start is not necessarily a planned piece of work. There may be a long run-in to the start of a new group, giving time to plan, but just as likely is a request for help from someone who is thinking of initiating a group without there being any warning. Part of the repertoire of a skilled professional is knowing both how to respond appropriately to an immediate request, and how to contribute to a more lengthy process. In either situation it can help to ask three questions:

- Who is starting the group?
- What is being started?
- How soon might it begin?

Who is starting the group?

First, it may help to reflect on who is making the first move. If the initiative has come from potential members, involvement may be very different from a situation where the professional is playing a major role in starting it off. A member of a visual impairment team had taken the lead and had initiated a group for deaf and blind people, finding it a difficult task. She made a long-term commitment to give in-depth help over a extended period.

> "You cannot just get people together and say, well, there you are, you wanted to meet each other, get on with it."　　　　*(Catherine, Rehabilitation Assistant)*

A colleague had helped another group, of younger visually impaired people, where the initiative had come, not from the professionals but from a young woman client. This time the team had acted much more as a short term practical resource.

> "We sent out her initial letters to people in the age group that she particularly wanted. So though she is actually going to be organising it, we have helped with the administration."　　　　*(Bet, Rehabilitation Officer)*

A group may be a shared initiative where both professional and member take the lead. An ex-patient of a cardiac ward at a hospital floated the idea of a group in the local paper and was joined by a nurse who had read the article.

> "I saw a letter in the paper asking for people to help, so I responded and have been involved ever since."　　　　*(Dora, Hospital Sister)*

Being clear about who is starting the group is an important first step, because the source of the initiative can have an effect on the way a professional is likely to be involved and the amount of time needed.

What is being started?

It is also important to be clear about what is being proposed. It will help to clarify whether it is a self help group run by its members that is being initiated or a professionally led support group. Or it might not be a group, but rather a self help service, controlled by people who have themselves experienced the situation, as described in Chapter 2. The role of the professional, the degree of commitment and the sort of advice and resources needed will vary according to what is really being proposed.

The list below summarises the characteristics of a self running group and can be used to help see what it is that is being started. Being aware of these characteristics will help a professional have a sense of vision of what a group might become, and so see what support is needed and where to hold back.

Checklist 7.1   Member-run self help groups
(based on Miller and Webb 1988)

☐   A shared sense of purpose

☐   Agreement on what behaviour is acceptable or not

☐   Enough structure to get things done

☐   Decision making and responsibilities shared between members

☐   A sense of identity and self worth

☐   Some external recognition

☐   Limits to the group recognised

☐   A sense that help can be sought without fear of being taken over

☐   Space for new members

☐   Members feel able to leave without the group's identity being threatened

☐   The group can opt to close if its reason for existing has come to an end

---

Groups may be closely connected with professional services or independent from the start. It may help to think of the group on a continuum.

AUTONOMOUS ———————— IN CONTACT ———————— INTEGRATED

Assess whether the group is likely to be autonomous from the start, simply in contact with a professional agency, or integrated into it to some degree. A group may plan to be self–running in the long run but closely connected to professional services initially, and its place on the continuum may change. It is not always possible to tell initially or to predict the future, but the likely relationship with an agency will affect both role and help given.

When might it begin?

Finally, it helps to know when a group might really start. It may be difficult to be precise, as the process of evolvement of a new self help group can be protracted and unpredictable. It is important for development to be at the pace that people feel is right for them, and for there to be plenty of time to think it through before any public action is taken.

Some professionals have used students on placement to help a new group. While this can be helpful, it can also bring problems. Student placements are designed to help an individual learn new professional skills and to fit in with the course they are taking. Placements are only for a few months or even a few weeks. It is unlikely that the timetable will fit neatly in to the unpredictable pattern of development of a new self help group. However, one way to use student time – and to help them learn about self help groups – may be to limit their contribution to a clearly defined task which is just one step in the process. The professional and the student work together, so the group does not have to establish a new relationship at the end of the placement. This avoids leaving an inexperienced student with the difficult job of helping a new self help group which may be beyond their ability.

Principles to bear in mind

There is no blueprint, but there is a set of general principles which should underpin the work of any professional working with a new self help group. They can be summarised under five headings:

- Offer support and encouragement
- Help to develop skills, ownership and confidence
- Build on and give access to proven good practice
- Diversify sources of support
- Undertake self-evaluation

Support and encouragement

People starting a new self help group are quite likely to be doing something they have never done before. Getting encouragement and support may be very important to them; not getting it may bring the whole initiative to a halt. Most people will have had experience of supporting friends and colleagues taking a new step in their career, or fostering young people's belief in themselves; in the same way one may encourage a new self help group. Members of groups easily distinguish between professionals who do support them and those who don't. Many group members talk with appreciation and warmth of professionals who have consistently encouraged them, but in contrast, a woman considering starting a group had had a bad experience when visiting her GP.

> "I had so wished there was someone to talk to who had gone through it when I was ill. I got better and began to think about starting a group. I tried to explain this to my GP and asked what she thought. She looked at me and said 'I can't think why you would want to do that.' I felt so put down."
>
> *(Eva, Skin Condition Group)*

Encouragement does not necessarily mean giving a wholesale, unquestioning welcome to an idea. It can involve asking questions, clarifying, helping people to think through their plans. However it is done, it is a first and important principle to take on board.

Developing ownership, skills and confidence

The principle of developing a sense of ownership, skills and confidence should underlie work with all new self help groups. If a group is to be run by members, ownership by its members must be the basis adopted from the very start. A hospital nurse, unaware of this, had unrealistically planned to do all the work herself. Her plans did not result in members running the group, because ownership from the beginning was with the professional, not the members.

> "I thought, well, I'll start the group and they can take it over when it gets going."
>
> *(Jo, Nurse)*

If there is no natural leader it can be very easy for the professional to take too much of a lead, and so lose the opportunity for the group to develop a sense of ownership. Liz Evans, a social worker, has written about her extensive experience working with groups of parents of children with disabilities. She came to see the significance of what she calls the 'central person in the group', either a founding member or a professional. Awareness of the significance of the way one works at the start for the group's future, she concluded, was crucial.

> "It is important if autonomy is to be achieved and members are fully committed to the group, that the 'central person' moves towards the sidelines and becomes more of an adviser and facilitator. This change should be the continuation of a process that begins with the first steps in setting up the group."
>
> *(Evans et al. 1986)*

Ownership of the group may be demonstrated by how decisions are taken, and who takes them. It can also be shown by the public image of the group. An inaugural meeting chaired by a member, for example, will demonstrate the nature of the group in a way not possible if a professional takes the chair.

> "We made a mistake, in hindsight. Ann offered to chair the meeting in the library and we gratefully accepted. She did it very well of course, she's experienced at that sort of thing, but it would have been better to have had a carer. It would have shown it was our group." *(Joan, Carers Group)*

It may be necessary for the professional to hold back, to decline to take a leading role, so that the process of ownership begins from the very start. Action by a professional should be consciously designed to help people increase a sense of ownership, skills and confidence. For example, it is possible to introduce two or three people to each other, to work with each other rather than one person with the professional. Positive feedback; helping people count up what they have achieved are the sorts of techniques needed. Holding back, though not always easy, may be right too, for example not going to the whole of every meeting.

There is no set procedure or protocol in such situations, but it helps to be aware of the significance of what is done and how quite small actions can help develop ownership, skills and confidence.

Good practice

Professionals helping a new self help group should work to a principle of discovering what other people have found to work, and giving the group access to this information. There is no need to reinvent the wheel, nor should people laboriously and perhaps painfully have to discover what works by making mistakes if this was not necessary. Passing on some broad principles of good practice could be very helpful, as set out in Checklist 7.2.

Checklist 7.2 Advice for new groups from other groups
(based on Miller and Webb, 1988)

❑ Have a committed core of people

❑ Set clear aims and objectives and requirements of membership

❑ Be aware of the limits of the group

❑ Achieve good publicity

❑ Keep interest going

❑ Work hard

❑ Don't expect to get everything done quickly

❑ Use outside support but with care, remaining in control and independent

❑ Learn how to deal with authorities

❑ Make outside contacts and decide how to use them

❑ Be assertive and determined

❑ Share responsibilities in the group

❑ Discuss problems openly

Local self help projects produce starterpacks which give more detailed advice. Rather than hand out advice yourself, it may be best to help people get access to publications themselves.

> "We had started a library for people using the mental health centre and included information about self help groups in it. So when Kit said he was thinking about starting a group, I was able to suggest he looked at the starterpack as a first step, and then get one himself." *(Petula, CPN)*

More specific advice may be obtainable from specialised national organisations and one way to work could be to find out what is available and ask for material to be sent to the group. Many national organisations produce guidelines: while some are very helpful, others are perhaps somewhat prescriptive and rigid. It also needs to be remembered that becoming associated with a national body is not right for every group.

> "We contacted the national organisation, but they insisted that we had to fundraise for them if we started as a local branch. No way were we doing that! So we decided to start as just a local group." *(Celia, Disability Group)*

There are advantages and disadvantages and this may need some thought. Checklist 7.3 sets out the issues:

Checklist 7.3   Help from national self help organisations

Advantages	Possible Limits
Give structure	May impose traditional way of organising
Publicity material	Help not sustained or long term
Link to other groups	May expect fundraising for them
Training and conferences	Small organisations, remote staff
Validate local group	Self help not main aim
Helpful publications	May require professional involvement

There are other ways too of giving people access to good practice. One can find out if there are neighbouring groups, based on the same issue which are already well-established. A visit, perhaps with transport arranged, could be a shortcut to both good practice and to increasing confidence. Seeing a model, talking to someone who has managed to set up their own group based on a similar issue, can be extraordinarily empowering. Local self help projects organise self help forums, giving local groups a chance to meet and for new groups to learn from those already well established.

Varied sources of help

A fourth principle is to aim to diversify sources of help. A group which looks to the professional as their sole source of support is much less likely to become autonomous and confident than one which has a number of organisations and individuals on which to draw. Working towards diversifying sources of help may be a gradual process or it could be part of the arrangement straightaway.

"I've had people come and ask where there might be premises available. And to see if I thought if the idea of a group was worthwhile. I tend to help with the premises, but from then on they really need to go to the self help co-ordinator."
(Angela, Health Visitor)

Most parts of the country will have a Council for Voluntary Service, a Community Council or a Volunteer Bureaux. Linking the group with one of these could be an early first step, especially if there is a specialist self help project. It may also be possible to establish long-term agency support for the group, rather than it coming simply from one individual. This has the advantages of consistency and stability, meaning that if the professional leaves or changes jobs, the group still gets support.

This principle, of diversifying sources of help, is however not easy to put into practice; too brisk a passing-over to other sources of help may lead to the group feeling unvalued. They may be able to accept help from someone they know and trust as an individual, but not from a strange source. On the other hand, unless it is appropriate to adopt a longterm 'backbone' role, described below, it may be essential to build in this principle from the start.

Self-evaluation

Finally, it is important to adopt self-evaluation of any support to a new group. This has two elements: monitoring what is being done, and evaluating it yourself. It may also be helpful to check out conclusions with a colleague, and to ask the group what they think.

The key to self-evaluation is keeping an account of what is done. If involved with a new group, write down what is done as the group develops. This helps to become clearer about the principles on which the work is being based and what roles are being played. An informal diary may be all that is needed, rather than a formal record, for these are not casenotes but a mechanism for helping the professional role to be effective. Keeping a record will help evaluate one's place in the group and to see how it might change. A community nurse working with a tranquilliser support group felt it was important that he had set out at the beginning to group members that he saw his job as helping them to function alone.

> "The amount I was involved changed to a second stage, they began to use me more to check out if what they were doing was OK. Now they are in the third stage, with more confidence in themselves. They occasionally invite me to come, but it is very much an invitation and I feel I am there as a guest."
>
> *(David, CPN)*

It is also possible to assess what is being done with a colleague or one's manager, or a self help project worker could help with the process. Ask the group, too, what they think, remembering that they are unlikely to be totally objective.

> "I asked the group if they wanted me to leave – but they were insistent that I stayed involved." *(Dora, Hospital Sister)*

In this case, it was appropriate to stay involved, though a change of role emerged, but group members may find it difficult to be objective, may not trust their own abilities enough to let a much appreciated professional go, and may fear that by appearing to reject their help, they will lose the contact. It is not enough just to ask the group but it need not be a complex operation. It is more a matter of common sense; making time; and having a system.

Roles to play

Self-evaluation may well lead to moving on to a different role. As well as working to the five principles outlined above, a professional needs to have a sense of what role they are playing, and to be aware of whether the role needs to change as time goes on. Seven broad roles are now outlined, some of which are followed up in more depth in the next chapter on support. Not all roles or the tasks within them are necessarily always appropriate; the trick is to play the one that is right for the time and the situation.

Catalyst

Catalysts start people thinking. They have an awareness of gaps in provision. They collect evidence. They are alert to people's emotional needs as well as to practical issues and to the potential of lay people's capacities. They ask questions. They are quick to see opportunities which could trigger off a new group: the ending of attendance at a day centre for example, or a time-limited course of lectures.

> "We set up a series of talks on infertility. The fifth week I think it was, someone from another self help group came to talk about how her group worked and offered help in setting one up if people were interested. We finished the last session early and people who wanted to set up a group stayed on."
>
> *(Alison, Social Worker)*

Catalysts also introduce people to each other, able to see that the contact between two like minded people might provide the impetus for a group. They don't feel the need to be the leader, or to take credit for what might happen.

Resource person

A resource person may either stay in the background or take on a more visible role. They provide practical resources: a meeting room, grants of money or help in kind, say typing and photocopying. They offer training, provide or suggest speakers and offer opportunities for publicity. They may offer the use of a telephone number for messages, or a drawer in a filing cabinet for storage. They give access to potential members, for example by sending out details of an inaugural meeting or by asking who would be interested.

The resource person is not always the direct provider of resources, rather they may give access to resources and encourage people to take advantage of them.

Link

Providing a link can be extraordinarily helpful to a new group. The link person puts someone in touch with a national organisation or a local self help project. They suggest local organisations, the names of helpful journalists or useful contacts within their organisation. They create paths through statutory organisations, aware of how complex the professional world can be for a new self help group.

> "I've written time and again and I can't get a reply. Nobody will even acknow-ledge the letter. It's hard to get a foot in the door."   *(Trish, Ileostomy Group)*

The link person connects new groups with the right person, identifies systems that can be used and gets access to them. They check the link is working well, from both perspectives. They also link potential new members together, finding ways to get over the issue of confidentiality.

> "The OT and the physiotherapist asked who would be interested, and gave their names to us, once they had given permission of course."
>
> *(Judith, Parents Group)*

Questioner

Questioners are not inquisitors. They do not take on an aggressive, intrusive role. Instead they clarify, they make people aware of issues which might never have occurred to them. They keep fundamental points to the fore. They ask, for example, what the group is setting out to achieve, who can come, and what the group's priorities will be.

> "I ask who the group is for and what its aims are. A professional can ensure that issues of membership and openness are integrated at the start of the group."   *(Murray, Social Worker)*

The questioner raises the need for groundrules to be set on confidentiality and on who gets time to speak. The questioner can help an equal opportunities perspective to be integrated into the group at its start. If they ask who the group is for, a group may become aware of whether they are making it possible for everyone to attend who might like to.

A good working relationship between a professional and an embryo group gives the opportunity not to tell people what to do but to ask questions which generally help clarify and illuminate. Questioning in an acceptable way shows that a group is valued rather than ignored.

Sustainer

Sustainers are there when they're needed. They may wait till they are asked for help or come forward with an offer of help when they see someone is flagging. They are trusted by the group, having taken the trouble to build up and maintain the contact. They appreciate the demands self-helpers may experience and the practical limits within which they have to work. Giving some practical help may be a form of sustaining. More often however, it is a question of being there to talk to.

> "She doesn't come to the meetings, but she gives us lots of advice."
>
> *(Kaneez, Single Parents Group)*

It can be an exhausting and depressing experience starting a new self help group, as well as being exhilarating and rewarding. Sustainers see initiators through bad patches, help them weigh up how much they have achieved so far and encourage them to continue.

Backbone

Backbones keep the group upright and on its feet. They take on a long-term commitment to the group, probably as part of their job. They play a major role in making sure the practical arrangements for meetings work – seeing that the room is open, the dates are publicised. They consciously play a link role between members, particularly introducing new ones to people who have been coming for some time. They give a perspective to group development, feeding in to the group for example, that it can be quite normal for any small group to go through a period of difficulty before settling down. They step in when members have unpredictable demands on their lives and cannot do the jobs for the group they had agreed to do. Backbones may have been the instigators of the group.

> "I started a group for people affected by Huntington's Disease, with a health visitor colleague, in response to requests from families to meet others. It's an isolating condition and very rare – you can't just put an advert in the paper. We were not leaders, and had to resist pressure to be so. It was a painful process at

first. We made a commitment that one of us would go to each group meeting
until the group decided otherwise."   *(Jill, Social Worker)*

The backbone role needs a lot of thought. The group can very easily become a
professionally led support group without careful appraisal of the role and it is
likely to be only occasionally appropriate.

Member

Some professionals are faced with the role of member, not always an easy part
to play.

> "I was an Ativan addict until I got in touch with the Tranx Release Group. I am a
> field social worker and our job is to help other people through their problems.
> Self help groups had always been for my 'clients', so taking this step needed me
> to swallow my pride and to change my attitude."
>
> *(Elizabeth, Social Worker)*

Members have experienced the same situation as others in the group. They
join in, giving and getting help in the same way as other members. They
choose to tell other members about their job or not, as they feel is right, but
if they do, they are clear to other members that they are there on the same
basis as everyone else.

> "I am a Health Visitor by profession and a member by circumstance, just like
> anyone else in the group."   *(Jo, Bereavement Group)*

Members who are also professionals may hold back from taking a leadership
role simply on the basis of their job, but may use their knowledge to help the
group when it is appropriate. Members set great store on confidentiality and
they are particularly aware of the potential complexity if one of their clients is
also a member of the group. They may, in the end, decide not to attend that
particular group if the juggling of roles is simply too much.

Difficulties to expect or avoid

Whatever the role, it is best to expect there to be difficulties and challenges
when helping a new self help group get going. Being aware of some of the
particular problems that may present themselves means one goes in fore-
warned, and perhaps able to avoid some problems.

Lack of skills and experience

First, lack of skills and experience may be a problem. Few professionals will have had training in working with self help groups, and only a handful will have been involved in enough groups to build up their skills through experience. Learning on the job and consciously acquiring knowledge may be necessary.

Some training may in fact be counter-productive for it may lead to a sense of professional standards and responsibility towards clients that are inappropriate in this setting. Standards proper to a professional service may not be right for a self help group, while a sense of responsibility towards clients may conflict with a principle of self determination.

Lack of experience may lead to a particular difficulty, that of not being able to assess quite what level of help to offer. Doing too much for a new group could lead it to become 'professionalised', running really as a professionally-led support group: doing too little leads to missed opportunities and self-helpers feeling undervalued.

Challenge to professional status

A handful of professionals may see the emergence of a new self help group as a challenge to their professional status, finding this hard to accept. As discussed in the previous chapter, a few groups may be confrontational, resulting in a group operating so far outside the culture of professional agencies that co-operation becomes unrealistic. More common, but also uncomfortable for some professionals, are new groups who wish to question existing practice or who raise questions about their colleagues.

Lack of time

Many professionals helping new self help groups are doing it on top of their normal job. Even with enormous goodwill, the competing demands of job and personal commitments may mean that it is not always possible to give the time that appears to be needed. This may not always be a bad thing: the group is realistic from the start about professional availability and there will be a limit to professional influence. Playing the backbone role, however, is likely to require dedicated time, the problem then being in allocating time or convincing a manager that it is a proper part of a job.

Planning time is also a problem, for one never knows when one might be needed. Even with a careful allocation of time when a group is being launched, it is not easy to know what will be needed later. Withdrawing too quickly can lead to as many difficulties as staying involved too long.

Difficult groups to start

Self help groups can be difficult groups to start, whoever is involved. Starting any small voluntary group is not necessarily easy, and the stages of 'forming, storming, norming and performing' *(Douglas 1978)*, normal in the formation of any group, are not always comfortable. Self help groups based on problems in people's lives bring particular challenges.

If a group just does not work, it may not be because the professional concerned has got it wrong for there could be a wide variety of reasons. The challenge here is to help people involved to retain their feelings of self worth and maintain good relationships with others and have a good ending. There may be a role too, not in starting the group, but in helping people decide not to go ahead after all.

Lack of support

Finally, support to the professional trying to help a group to start may be unavailable. It is all too easy to continue working in any difficult situation without acknowledging the need for support. It may be necessary to look outside the professional agency, for it may not be so much supervision that is needed as easy access to a commonsense outsider, who provides an opportunity to talk in confidence and helps to clarify the process.

Being alert to these various difficulties will help to avoid some of them in the first place, and to accept that some of them may be quite normal.

An alternative approach

This chapter has concentrated so far on situations where a professional is involved to a greater or lesser extent in a specific group. It ends with a suggestion of a quite different approach: energies and resources may in fact be better used in creating an atmosphere in which self help groups can flourish, rather than in direct work with individual groups. This is likely to need an agency policy rather than an individual approach and will require a fair amount of self-assessment, planning and some resources. If taking this approach, assess the usefulness for the development of self help groups of the following resources:

- The building and meeting rooms
- Library and information resources
- Events and speakers

The building   Access to meeting rooms, and letting people know that they can be used is the first point to consider. Is there a meeting room that could be used by a self help group? It would need to be private, comfortable and accessible to people with disabilities. People using it will need to have access to suitable toilets and to a kitchen. It should be possible to use the room without having to have a professional present. Booking arrangements, including the possible cost need to be clear. The length of time it can be booked for, both for specific meetings and over what period of time has to be thought through. Parking for disabled people might be needed too. It is not enough that the room can be used, its availability has to be publicised – and re-publicised after some time. If there is possible competition with use by professional activities, there must be an honest appraisal and rules about this. Whatever is agreed must be honoured.

Library and information resources   There may be a library of information that could help people starting self help groups. It may be that its function is broader, helping people to learn about the conditions with which they are coping as much as about running groups *(Sumner 1994)*. Professional agencies with information resources made available to users of their services are demonstrating that they value people's own knowledge and wish to extend it, and want to encourage them to take action.

An accessible shelf of useful books and a collection of articles may be enough if an entire library is impracticable; either may include information about starting self help groups and accounts about them. Reading about other people's experience of setting up self help groups can be a powerful trigger.

Events and speakers   Thought should be given to initiating events or inviting speakers from existing self help groups. As well as reading about groups, hearing a self help group member speak can begin the process of initiating a group. It also demonstrates that the agency values what groups do and that it is willing to learn from their experience. Or it may be possible to invite group members to events about research or treatment designed primarily for professionals, which makes group members feel valued.

All three resources – availability of rooms, access to a library and opportunity to hear speakers – may be seen as 'pre-self help group work', as early stages of a development. While they are forms of support, more importantly they will provide triggers to future development and investing in these can be a fruitful and important preliminary step. This approach would need to go alongside providing a variety of support to new self help groups; creating a favourable climate, an atmosphere in which self help and mutual aid is valued and can flourish, may be a complementary rather than an alternative approach.

Summary

- Be clear about who is starting the group, what is being suggested and when it might begin.

- Adopt principles on which work should be based.

- Clarify what roles are appropriate to play and be aware of how these may need to change.

- Be aware of difficulties that may be encountered and consider getting support.

- Consider taking a deliberately new approach: the creation of an atmosphere in which self help can flourish.

8 Supporting

Helping groups once they are established can be as important as giving a hand when they begin, for professionals can still have a role to play once the group is up and running. The question of the right balance is again an important thread running through this chapter. These two chapters, 7 and 8, are best read as a pair rather being seen as two completely different ways of working for a division of 'supporting' and 'starting off' as two apparent separate ways of working with self help groups is to some extent a false divide.

Four issues are covered here: identifying starting off points for supporting established self help groups; principles which should inform the relationship at this stage, including the recognition that there may be no professional role to play; examples of how to support groups, and the limits to support.

Starting off points

When it is right to offer support, two rather different starting off points can be identified. In some situations, a professional may continue a process of contact and support to a group which they helped as it began, and where stepping back is under way. In other situations, a professional comes fresh to a group already established to a greater or lesser extent, and with which no contact existed in its early stages. The relationship and what might be appropriate ways to work may be very different in the two settings.

Stepping back from a new group

Stepping back from a new group is an issue where the experience of Liz Evans will again be helpful. She stresses the need to move more to becoming an adviser and facilitator if the group is to be self-running, and to build steps towards this into work in the early days. If this has been possible, a second stage of supporting a group will be a natural progression for both the professional and group members. A number of issues will have been flagged up, people will have been alerted and reminded of a future change in role well in advance. Stepping back will have been timed to coincide with what the group feels is right for them *(Evans et al. 1986)*.

This gradual change of role is possible and can work provided it is built in from the very beginning, done gradually if needed and carried out in consultation with the group. A form of 'tough love' may be needed, for it may be necessary to balance what the group is saying they want with what is really needed for them to achieve autonomy in the long term. Alternatively, the professional may find they need to accept direction from the group; it may be that members make it clear that they would prefer less professional involvement rather sooner than might have been expected. This should be seen as achievement rather than rejection.

If this gradual change in role, from being closely involved to being an occasional supporter has not been worked through from the very beginning, there may be a need to introduce a bridging period, consciously and over a period of time. It is not good practice to make changes without consultation and warning and too quick a change can lead to a group ending unnecessarily. A timetable, planned changes in role and reduced frequency of contact will all need thought and have to be discussed with the group.

Backing up an established group

A different context is a situation where support is being given to an established group, without there having been any involvement with it when it began. This may be because a professional is new in post, or inherits the contact from a colleague. It may be that the group has got in touch with a professional agency and asked for support. In either case there is no history, a situation which both brings challenges and eases the relationship.

It brings challenges for the professional of getting to know the group and the individuals within it and of creating a new relationship. There will be issues for the group too. Members will need to get to know a new person. Some members, as individuals, may be clients or patients of the professional. Now their relationship is also as members of an established group. Any difficulties for either group members or professional may be quickly overcome, but in

some situations a period of transition will be needed. It will be particularly important for the professional to get to know the group, for effective support cannot be given without knowing how it works and who is involved.

This starting off point may actually be easier than a situation where there has been heavy involvement with the group in the past. There will not be the need to extricate oneself or to change relationships so much. It is possible to come in with a fresh eye, careful as a newcomer not to give an opinion too forcefully, but seeing a fresh viewpoint as a strength which may well benefit the group.

Principles to work to

The principles that should lie behind supporting established groups overlap with those suggested for working with new groups. Checklist 8.1 summarises what principles might inform practice: use the list to clarify the professional role and to see how it might need to change or end as a group develops.

Checklist 8.1   Principles of support to established groups

❑   Help develop skills, ownership and confidence

❑   Build on and give access to proven good practice

❑   Diversify sources of support

❑   Offer support and encouragement

❑   Undertake self-evaluation of the professional role

❑   Do nothing and hold back offers of support if appropriate

❑   Ensure groups have a real choice on accepting help or not

---

How close a group is to a professional agency will influence how significant each of these principles are. The first five principles, also part of working with new groups, will be specially relevant when an established group remains in close association with an agency, while a group which is moving to becoming highly autonomous is likely to have different needs; then the principle of doing nothing may be the right one. The first five principles were discussed in the previous chapter, the last two, explored here are likely to apply more to working with established groups than those in the early stages.

Holding back

If a group has asked for help, the professional responds knowing that their involvement is likely to be welcomed. The situation where support is offered by the professional is rather different. In deciding whether to offer support or not, it may be well to think first if any intervention at all is appropriate. A lay voluntary group may not appear to be working in the same efficient way as a group led by a professional might be, for example, but it is possible that offering support is an attempt to transfer a professional model to a lay group.

> "The group may be just a bit vague, a bit naff. The perception of the group member and the professional can be different."   *(Murray, Social Worker)*

Once one has accepted a principle of ownership by the group themselves as the basis for self help groups, then whatever the situation, the professional may just have to hold back. It may be a difficult problem involving a clash of personalities which no outsider can influence.

> "We haven't gone in to help but I think they need it because it's a self-destruct line they are on at the moment." "But isn't that for the group to sort out themselves? It's their self help group. The move should be within."
> *(Chris and Angela, Health Visitors)*

Recognising there may no longer be a role at all is also important. Once a group is self-running, the supportive role may no longer be right. This then leaves the professional part largely as one of putting people in touch or promoting groups, the subject of the next chapter.

Accepting the right of the group to choose

A group that is starting may of course also choose whether or not to accept an offer of help, but it is much more likely to be an issue once the group has become established. Declining the use of professional resources may be part of the group moving to greater autonomy.

> "As soon as we've got the money, we're off!"   *(Denise, Drugs Group)*

Where members have a strong sense of self–determination, they will set the boundaries while retaining a good working relationship. A group spoke warmly about their contacts with a hospital but did not involve its staff in managing the group.

"The committee runs the group, all amputees and carers. We have no professionals on the committee at all." *(Cheryl, Amputees Group)*

How to support

Putting people in touch with groups and promoting groups can also be forms
of support, but if more than this is needed, then a range of tried and tested
methods can be used:

- Offering practical resources
- Giving talks or finding speakers
- Attending meetings and events
- Being available in the background
- Helping members develop skills
- Working together on a project

Offering practical resources

There may well be practical resources within a professional organisation that
could be useful to a self help group. Offering them may save groups money,
effort and time and show that what they are doing is valued.

"The group was finding the actual production of the newsletter too big a job, so I
asked my secretary if she could fit it in for a bit." *(Valerie, Consultant Psychiatrist)*

A variety of resources provided by professionals have all proved useful to self
help groups. Use Checklist 8.2 on the next page to see if any of these apply.
Many groups appreciate practical help of this kind but others may see it as a
form of interference. It is important that the group can feel free to choose.

"The support group began at the hospital but we don't meet there any more. We
had speakers and some of the professionals were quite interested and would
come as well. Some people thought, well, if they are going to be there, I'm not
going to be there. It put a lot of people off. So we meet in a room above a pub."
(Vicky, Parents Group)

Although problems like this can occur, in general the offer of practical resources
is a helpful way to support groups and is appreciated by many.

Checklist 8.2   Practical support to self help groups

❑   Meeting rooms and coffee

❑   Photocopying and typing

❑   Speakers at meetings

❑   Use of notice boards

❑   Use of internal mailing systems

❑   Places to hold fundraising events

❑   Access to grants

❑   Storage for group library and files

❑   Mailing address and place for phone messages

❑   Transport to meetings

Giving talks or finding speakers

Groups vary in how relevant they see the contribution of outside speakers. Some find it inappropriate to invite professional speakers at all, feeling that the group is about sharing experiences and information between themselves. The professional 'expert' can dilute this aspect of the group's activities. Others, either occasionally or on a regular basis, welcome talks. Members can find it helpful to be updated on current research on the medical condition on which their group is based, to learn more about services and benefits and to hear about complementary therapies. A panel of speakers, with group members raising questions is often successful and blurs the distinction between the expert speaker and the lay member. Large groups, where discussion is less practicable often adopt the pattern of speakers, singly or on a panel, as a feature of most meetings.

Groups rarely offer fees, except to a private practitioner, but usually offer expenses to all speakers. Many speakers decline these or give the money to a charity, but professionals should feel that they can accept expenses and that that scale of money is not usually a problem for a group.

Groups can, however, find it difficult to get speakers. Groups who have speakers frequently, or cover a rural area may find it a particular problem. One obstacle is getting access. A group may well appreciate suggestions of people to approach and perhaps the offer of an initial approach to find out if the person concerned is willing to be asked. Small groups may think they

cannot invite someone to speak to a handful of members, and may welcome offers or suggestions of easing the approach to a colleague. If an offer like this is made to a group, it is best made informally, in such a way that the group can take it up or not, so that they feel under no pressure to accept.

One difficulty can arise from speakers who are more used to addressing a professional audience, than a group of people themselves experiencing the problem which forms the topic of the talk.

> "We had a consultant come to speak and I was really quite disappointed because it seemed to me he was giving a talk that he had given to some other doctors, or students. A lot of it was in jargon. At times he was talking about 'they'. He did pull himself up once, said 'that was you', but it was almost as if he'd forgotten where he was."
>
> *(Meg, ME Group)*

Few speakers would make such a mistake, but it can be challenging to talk to a group and some guidelines may help to get it right. Use Checklist 8.3 if asked to give a talk to a group.

Checklist 8.3   Giving talks to self help groups

❑ Agree how long the talk should be (20 minutes may be enough)

❑ Find out if there are other speakers too

❑ Agree on questions – whether they are welcomed, and any boundaries that need to be set

❑ Ask if they need the speaker to stay for the whole meeting or to come for only part of it. People may want to talk over coffee and raise issues they felt unable to ask about in the meeting; or the group may want time on their own

❑ Make sure the venue for the meeting is clear, arrangements for parking and any other practical matters are decided. Ask for a map if this would help

❑ Think in advance about equipment and ask if it is available. Audio-visual aids may not always be available or appropriate

❑ Get a balance between avoiding jargon and technical language and not speaking down to the audience

❑ Agree on any financial arrangements in advance

The benefits that come from speaking at a meeting are not one way. Going as a speaker gives a chance to get to know the group and to learn more about the issue on which it is based from a new perspective.

Attending meetings and events

Being a speaker gives a role and a chance to attend without long-term involvement. In some groups, professionals attend meetings more regularly, the arrangement working well in some cases, but in others being an intrusion. Check with the group what they feel about outsiders' attendance and review arrangements at regular intervals. Both groups and professionals can welcome the opportunity that comes for individual members to get easy access to professional advice in an informal setting.

> "The clinical psychologist may have a quiet word with a distraught member."
> *(Barry, Back Pain Group)*

> "We find the nurses like to come because they are going to be asked questions. You see someone sat in the corner with their shoes and socks off, but he doesn't like to go to the clinic in case it's nothing." *(Jeff, Diabetic Group)*

The benefit may not always be for individual members: being at the meeting can mean that a problem to do with the group, rather than individuals, can be solved on the spot.

Some groups have 'open meetings', deliberately planned and publicised so that people who want to find out more about their work can come, knowing that they will be welcome. These work well, giving the opportunities for interaction and contact without intrusion. Open meetings can be suggested as a mechanism to a group whose members want more contact but fear that the presence of professionals will hold back the process of sharing experiences in a normal meeting.

Going to a fundraising event can work well. Groups which put on fundraising events at a hospital, day centre and so on find them successful, not only for the money they raise but for the opportunity of informal contact with staff who come to buy or who contribute in some way. Just baking a cake can show the group they are valued.

Occasionally a group may invite a professional to be an honorary president, involving attendance simply at an annual meeting. A small number of self help groups have professionals as committee members, so they attend committee and full meetings automatically. Being more actively involved on a committee or attending meetings regularly will give the opportunity to act as an adviser.

Advisers offer an outsider's perspective. They point out how people outside the group might perceive it. They suggest options for what the group might do. They try to avoid being identified with any faction that may develop in a group, so they can be approached by anyone. They act as an intermediary if needed. They may give credibility, but not directional control.

When attending meetings it is important to have an awareness of the role that is being played, which may be as adviser or more likely, as a guest – or a combination of both. A professional presence may be difficult for members who find it intimidating.

> "When I first got on that committee, I wouldn't open my mouth. He scared me to death. I still feel a bit intimidated by him now."
>
> *(Pamela, Tranquilliser Support Group)*

Be aware that professional presence at meetings can bring problems as well as advantages to the group. There may be other ways to help, seeing key members outside meetings for example.

Being available in the background

An easier role may be to be available in the background. Even well run and long established groups can appreciate contact with a professional who knows their group, but stays in the background. This gives the chance to call on advice when the group feels they need it and is usually an informal but often very helpful relationship, though the title of adviser is unlikely to be used and the whole approach may need to be low-key.

In a few groups, the role may be formalised. A professional advisory panel is required by at least one national organisation and in one local area the adviser role was developed as a logical and effective way of helping mental health groups to become more independent.

> "A couple of groups now have a named clinical adviser. We instigated a number of groups, but one of the problems was that people were very reluctant to let us go. One way of facilitating access to us was to have an adviser so they could talk to us without us having control." *(Rob, CPN)*

Helping members develop their skills

Part of the advisory role can include helping people in self help groups develop their skills and confidence. There are also some other ways in which professionals can help: short courses or training sessions, for example, on subjects like listening skills, assertiveness, relaxation and giving talks. It may be possible for a professional to offer to run these.

A coaching role may be needed. Group members invited to give talks about their group, for example, may want to rehearse and go through what they are going to say on an individual basis. Conferences or training events put on by other organisations may be useful for groups and it may be that professionals can help find sources of money to meet the cost. The trick is to aid the process of developing skills without dictating to the group what they should do or over-formalising what is done.

Working together on a project

Another way of supporting a group is to work together on a project rather than being involved in the whole range of group activities. This approach can avoid too much involvement, bring the chance for contact and mean that time-limited help can be offered. One example is co-editing a publication.

> "The chair of our group and the consultant were joint authors. We've now got a very helpful booklet for parents on how best to cope with their child's asthma, combining both viewpoints." *(Jane, Asthma Group)*

Other examples are group activities, for example a parents' group successfully organised a summer playscheme for children of families in the group, drawing on help from social workers in the first year, but running it themselves in subsequent years. The actual project will not be the only end result. Projects give opportunities for interaction, for professionals and group members to get to know each other and for people to develop their skills.

The organising skills required are not those necessarily included in professional training. The role may not be so much as professional expert, but as friend of the group, prepared to join in and learn on the job.

The limits to support

There are limits to the support that a professional can give a self help group. Support is affected by:

- Lack of continuity and change of jobs
- Limits of time and energy
- The limits of support by any outsider to initiatives run by the people concerned

Lack of continuity

Self help groups value and benefit from continuity of relationships with professionals in health and social services. Members take part as volunteers, putting in time to their group as and when they can. It takes time to build up a relationship and can require a great deal of effort to rebuild it if the key professional concerned moves on. With so many changes in both health and social services, as well as natural movement of staff, lack of continuity in professional agencies has to be recognised as a real problem for groups which limits the extent to which professional help assists their work.

Lack of continuity can also be frustrating for the professionals concerned. A consistent relationship, in contrast, will be satisfying and give more time for liaison and support to voluntary groups, as one professional who gave a lot of time to parents' groups found.

> "I've worked in this area for 16 years. The children who I knew as children are now having babies. I am at ease with my caseload."   *(Alison, Health Visitor)*

Lack of continuity in groups can also make giving support difficult. Contact people in groups often change, particularly where the issue on which the group is based is one where people are in a stage of transition, and so need to move on from a group for personal reasons. It is part of the nature of some self help groups for there to be change and new people coming in can be a strength. For professionals, having taken time to carefully build up contacts it can be very frustrating. Ideally, part of good practice by groups should be to make sure there is careful handover and introductions. In practice, this does not always happen.

In both situations – lack of continuity among professionals and in groups – a realistic approach is needed, regarding this as part of the relationship. It should not be used however as an excuse to rush developing a relationship or to detach oneself too soon. Managers should be aware of the risk of losing all the benefit of carefully nurtured contacts if they insist on staff stopping their support too quickly. Some forms of support to self help groups require consistency and at times, a long-term commitment. Lack of consistency of support can be interpreted as a professional not taking the group seriously. If long-term support simply is not possible, then it may be more honest to say this at the beginning, rather than build up expectations that are dashed.

Limits of time and energy

Members of groups appreciate competing demands that professionals have on their time. Some would prefer time to be spent on giving care to individuals than to the group, if there has to be a choice. Others are less sure, feeling that lack of time is an excuse rather than a reason for not keeping in touch with groups and supporting them. Competing demands, whatever the truth of the matter, are a constraint on time available for supporting groups and the contract culture, with pressure to deliver agreed outcomes may make this even more difficult.

The limits on time are to some extent elastic if the professional concerned sees their contact with a group as a form of informal community involvement, even a form of voluntary work. While some professionals are quite happy with this way of working, there can be pros and cons. Some groups feel that it is taking advantage of the goodwill of individuals and that time should be formalised.

> "They are busy, they have families and commitments too. Why should they do something for nothing? It's got to be in the job description, part of the mainstream." *(Sandra, Twins Group)*

From a practical point of view, many groups meet in the evenings. Attending meetings means working outside conventional working hours, resulting in extra unpaid work or negotiating time-off-in-lieu. Managers need to be aware of such practical matters; this is an issue needing to be dealt with by the agency rather than by the individual concerned. Lack of recognition of pressures that can result from working with self help groups, on top of a normal workload, can lead to people feeling overburdened.

Support as an outsider

Any support from someone outside a group is limited by the fact that they are an outsider. This is not just in the field of self help groups, but has to be recognised by anyone intervening in organisations which concern those involved, not those outside. If the two worlds of the professional and the self help group are far apart, then this limit has to be recognised as a important constraint and accepted as such. If the two worlds are close or coincide, then it will be less of a problem.

To conclude this chapter, remember again that there may be no role at all for professionals in supporting groups directly. It may be enough to put people in touch with them and to concentrate on getting that right. In some situations however it is likely that some supportive role can be useful and at times it can be highly significant in helping a group develop and fulfil its potential.

Summary

- Identify the starting point for support.

- Adopt principles on which work should be based.

- Hold back offers of support if appropriate.

- Accept the right of the group to choose whether to accept support or not.

- Choose from a range of possible actions.

- Be aware of the limits to support.

9 Promoting

So far we have talked about ways of working directly with self help groups. There are other ways of assisting them which are less direct and one of these might be described as promoting them. Professionals may wonder whether this is really their job, but experience suggests that it can be. Promotion overlaps with the concepts of support and of putting people in touch, but should be considered separately.

Promotion can involve a professional in varying roles: publicist, door-opener and product champion. In this chapter, I discuss reasons why professionals might take on these roles; suggest guidelines to which to work; and outline action to consider taking. The differences between the lone champion in an organisation and a committed agency, where all staff may be involved are discussed. Dilemmas and challenges to be faced, accepted or dealt with are again explored. This area of work is not for everyone, however, and not all professionals may become involved.

Why promote self help groups?

First think why professionals might consider actively promoting self help groups, either groups generally, or publicising individual groups. Taking a broad approach, it can be seen as a logical part of a whole web of support and encouragement. Promotion is a way to be pro-active in giving support. Looking into it in more detail, there are a number of more specific reasons why promoting self help groups can be part of good professional practice:

- To be a partner in a three-pronged approach
- To put a theory of joint working with voluntary groups into practice
- As an indirect way of putting people in touch with groups
- As a low-key method of support

An active partner

Members of self help groups often make considerable efforts to make their group known, putting in time and using the resources of the group to acquire and distribute publicity material. "You've got to go out and sell yourself," members often say. It is not always easy, though, for members to market themselves if the issue which has brought them together in the first place is one which restricts energy and time. The issue may be a very sensitive one, needing confidentiality rather than personal exposure. And while a group might have a very effective publicity officer for a time, if they move on, there may be no-one else to take it on.

A more profitable way to approach the issue of promoting groups is to see it as needing a three-pronged approach, not being just the job of the groups. Groups themselves want to and should take on some responsibility, but it is unrealistic to expect all the resources needed to be found within them; nor is it always logical to do it alone for reasons of scale.

Groups form the first prong of a three-pronged approach. A second prong should be promotion by the voluntary sector. A self help project, a CVS, a Volunteer Bureau or a specialist umbrella agency are well placed to undertake broad promotional activities with and for a range of self help groups.

Professionals can provide the third prong, either alone or working as an active partner with group members or with a voluntary sector organisation. With concerted effort, rather than groups struggling alone, some of the problems that limit effective promotion can be overcome. Self help groups will then become much more visible – and hence more accessible to people who might need them.

Public demonstration

A second reason for promoting self help groups is to demonstrate a belief in what groups do publicly, to implement a theory of joint working with voluntary groups. Promoting groups shows the groups themselves that the organisation wants to endorse their work. It is also a public demonstration – noticeboards and displays in a health or social services agency tell the visitor something about the organisation's policies and community links.

"While waiting to see a colleague in another agency, I had a chance to read their noticeboard. It was full of useful information about local voluntary groups, attractively presented. I could see their team had close links and felt that the organisation valued what they did."   *(Mary, Social Worker)*

Indirect linking

A third reason for taking on promotion as part of good practice is so that people can learn about groups without having to go through a professional. Many methods suggested in this chapter will provide an indirect method for putting people in touch with them. People may want the information but not to have to get it directly from a professional.

A form of support

A last reason for promoting self help groups is to give support. Many initiatives by professionals are appreciated by group members, not just for their practical usefulness but as a clear demonstration to the groups themselves that their work is valued. A theme of this book is the powerful effect of support on helping groups to start and to keep going; promoting groups is a way to give support without intruding.

The experience of a group whose members felt that their work was not valued shows how important it can be to groups to have evidence of support rather than rejection.

"When I asked my GP's surgery to display a notice, they sent me a letter back, saying that three of the doctors thought 'it was not appropriate to display the leaflet.' I was angry. I would have admired them much more if they had said, come in and tell us what you do. Anyway, at an event last week at the community centre, we had a display and I asked a GP and the practice manager, who were both there, to come and see it and we talked about the group. Well, now tell me why you wouldn't put my leaflet up, I said. She just looked at me and said, will you forgive us, because we were wrong and I thought – that's made my day."   *(Lucy, Tranx Group)*

Guidelines to consider

Consider adopting some broad guidelines, set out in Checklist 9.1. A mixture of theory and practice, some may appear self evident but are based on mistakes that might have been avoided as well as on success.

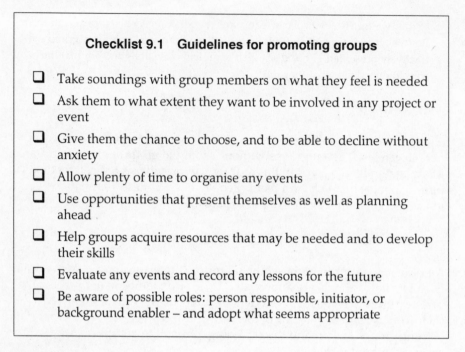

Checklist 9.1   Guidelines for promoting groups

❑ Take soundings with group members on what they feel is needed

❑ Ask them to what extent they want to be involved in any project or event

❑ Give them the chance to choose, and to be able to decline without anxiety

❑ Allow plenty of time to organise any events

❑ Use opportunities that present themselves as well as planning ahead

❑ Help groups acquire resources that may be needed and to develop their skills

❑ Evaluate any events and record any lessons for the future

❑ Be aware of possible roles: person responsible, initiator, or background enabler – and adopt what seems appropriate

Actions to take

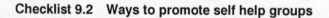

Choose the method of promotion which is right for the professional agency and the groups. Promotion can mean taking any of a range of activities, summarised in Checklist 9.2.

Checklist 9.2   Ways to promote self help groups

❑ Put up and use noticeboards

❑ Mount special displays

❑ Use national 'weeks'

❑ Make arrangements for groups to visit wards and courses

❑ Invite groups to give talks

❑ Mount fundraising or publicity events

❑ Include in databases, handbooks or information points

❑ Undertake research

Noticeboards

First take stock, then move on to thinking what might be done in the future, using Checklist 9.3.

Checklist 9.3   Making use of noticeboards

❑ What is the purpose of noticeboards in the agency?

❑ How many, what type and what use is made already?

❑ How attractive and accessible are they to people coming in?

❑ Who has responsibility for keeping them up to date?

❑ Are extra ones needed, and should they be dedicated to community information?

❑ Are locked glass-fronted boards needed or simple pinboards?

❑ What size and how many are needed?

❑ What system for putting posters and notices up might be appropriate (e.g. checking with a receptionist)?

❑ What standard of material is expected?

❑ Who might take responsibility for acquiring information and keeping it tidy and up to date?

❑ Are there graphics skills to draw on to help make displays and posters attractive and eye-catching?

Promoting groups through the use of noticeboards may just need some fine tuning to systems that are in place already. Alternatively, approach it as a project requiring assessment, plans and resources. A student might include it as part of a placement or a couple of team members take it on as their responsibility. Once seen as a project, then resources may be less of a problem and time will be properly allocated.

Displays

Displays, while achieving some of the same objectives, are normally temporary. They are best planned to be put up as part of a larger activity such as a conference, a study day or open day or to mark a special theme for a week or a day.

The standard of a display is important: a home-made effect makes people switch off, while too glossy an appearance may be wrong for informal groups. Some groups may be able to get the loan of good display material from their national organisation. It may be possible to link them up with a graphics section in an organisation for help and resources. A League of Friends or a local charitable fund might be approached for grants of money for new publicity material.

Think whether a display should be staffed or unstaffed. A major event may justify asking group members to staff a display for at least part of a day, but on the whole, it is best to plan an unstaffed display, with leaflets for people to take away, and a book or box for enquiries. It is dispiriting for people to give their time as volunteers and then not be used. Only when a reasonable number of enquirers can be predicted should group members be asked to staff a display.

If a display is large enough to be called an exhibition, there can be other opportunities. A well-known person can be asked to come and open it. This makes it news and a press release can then be sent out. General awareness about the group or the subject can be heightened by posters advertising the exhibition, even if people don't come to see it.

National 'weeks'

It is common practice for there to be national weeks for some major issues: carers, back pain or Alzheimer's Disease, for example. Professionals whose work relates to the subject of a national week have an easy method to promote self help groups within the context of a wider range of needs and services. 'Weeks' provide an opportunity to build links with the local group and plan an event together. Joint working with the group can be a good learning experience and demonstrate co-operation.

There may be no need to be proactive, just to make a positive response. A back pain group, for example asked staff to put up a display for a week in the waiting area for the out-patient orthopaedics clinic in Back Pain Week, but by taking the initiative, it may be possible to open doors for a group. The local radio station or the local paper might well be interested in a feature. A 'week' is news, providing a peg on which to hang publicity. Suggest to journalists that group members are interviewed or encourage the group to take the initiative.

Visits to wards and centres

Promotion is not just about publicity: the actual presence of group members on a hospital ward, or as visitors to a clinic, a course or day centre, can be an effective way of promoting their work without requiring major resources.

"The group has mushroomed since the hospital visiting has become well established. It's more likely, in my experience, that people will join the group if they
have met another member when they're in hospital."   *(Dora, Hospital Nurse)*

Visiting needs careful thought, planning and monitoring, all of which need
time. The reason for group members visiting should be worked out and
agreed between the group and the staff. All staff need to understand this and
to make group members welcome, for depending on one key person being on
duty will not work. It may work for the group to take on a simple regular task,
making the tea at a rehabilitation course, for example, which means they have
a presence as well as giving a short talk about the group. Formal training is
not needed, but proper briefing is necessary.

"We tried it with the social workers giving some training, but it made people
stilted, they became less themselves and there was a risk of overlap with our job.
Now we've developed some informal guidelines on what to avoid and this works
well. I make sure I keep in touch and act as liaison between the group and the
ward."   *(Dora)*

If regular visits are not practicable, groups may be willing to come in when
asked. Individuals may want to meet someone before they leave – group
members may be very happy to call in and tell them about the group. Proper
preparation and agreement on their role will still be needed, for arriving and
being made to feel unwelcome is very discouraging.

Invite groups to give talks

Regular staff meetings offer opportunities to invite members of groups to
come in and talk about their activities. It works best for the initiative to be
taken by the professional, rather than expecting a group to find out about and
get access to meetings. Most groups will be glad of the opportunity.

Be clear about why they are being invited, and agree arrangements well in
advance, following the guidelines in Checklist 5.5 (page 47). Avoid making a
vague offer, which is then not followed up.

Special events

As well as displays, and activities for 'weeks', there is evidence that professionals and groups have successfully arranged a range of special events.
These can be extraordinarily successful in promoting both the idea of self help
and the work of individual groups.

"We've had two Self Help Carnivals now, supporting the groups who took over the grounds and running our own Open Day alongside their activities. The Carnivals have reached more of our staff than any number of training courses could ever hope to do."   *(Heather, Hospital Chief Executive)*

While even an evening needs careful planning, time and resources, less ambitious schemes can work well too, focusing on particular areas of interest and targeting interested people.

"We planned a special evening together, with talks, displays and discussion. 'Birth and beyond' involved people from the hospital, the community and all the self help groups."   *(Jo, Midwife)*

Include in information

In some situations, professionals are required to give out information. The Children Act (1989) for example, says that parents of children with special needs must receive information on what services are available. Other guidelines, such as the Patients Charter encourage provision of information, and most professionals would see this as part of good professional practice.

A range of opportunities may be available for providing systematic written information, listed in Checklist 9.4. When these become part of procedures, staff do not have to be specially briefed, nor do they have to remember to pass on information. Systems for providing written information complement personal conversations with individuals, rather than replace them. While this is only one way to put people in touch with groups, it is a significant and effective way of promoting them and one much appreciated by group members.

Checklist 9.4   Opportunities for giving information

❑   List established groups in handbooks
❑   Include group information in letters about appointments
❑   Make details part of discharge information
❑   Feature groups in newsletters
❑   Advertise self help projects on outpatient appointment cards

---

Undertake research

Professionals can promote groups by undertaking research about them. While unlikely to be the prime reason for planning and doing research, it is evident that even a small research project can make groups more visible and better understood.

> "The physiotherapist at the Child Development Centre was doing research and was an absolute whizzkid on dyspraxia. She was wonderful for us. We got 40 members ever so quickly."   *(Lyn, Dyspraxia Group)*

Research does not only result in individual groups becoming more accessible to people who might join. It can help clarify the different roles of self help groups and professionals, gives the group some standing and makes members feel valued. The overall impact is promotion of both the idea of self help and of particular groups concerned.

Product champion or agency commitment?

Some methods of promoting groups can be undertaken by a single enthusiast, others need the commitment of a whole team or even a whole organisation. Consider what is possible for an individual worker to do, and what can only be done as part of a committed team.

Agency commitment

A large-scale event, a hospital Open Day and Self Help Carnival for example, would need the backing of both senior management and a substantial number of staff. A long process of changing attitudes and learning about self help groups may be needed before some of the suggestions in this chapter can be implemented. There has to be both a sense of the time being ripe and there being supportive individuals in key positions.

The benefit may not only be to the groups. Some of the ideas suggested may also be useful ways for an agency to put current policies into practice or meet legal requirements. It may be possible to achieve professional goals at the same time as benefiting groups.

The product champion

Work by individuals may however also be very important and be part of a process of change. Professionals committed to self help groups and their potential contribution can speak up about how they feel and share positive experiences. They may be the only one in a team. A CPN was one of very few people in a mental health team who felt this way and who acted as a product champion. He took opportunities to challenge what he thought were limited views whenever possible.

> "Some people say 'they don't know what they are doing.' 'They don't have the training and I can do it better.' 'If people are not qualified, it can't be valuable.' I always make comments back to the contrary."   *(David, CPN)*

Taking opportunities to promote groups privately helps colleagues and students to understand more about how groups work and means that incorrect statements are discussed. Being a lone champion can feel an isolated position, out on a limb, but their work can have immense impact on long-term change to attitudes – and hence, in time, to changes in practice.

Dilemmas and difficulties

It is possible for any professional to promote self help groups successfully. There will also of course be dilemmas and difficulties: endorsement of groups, discussed in detail in Chapter 6, is an important issue; there will always be a problem of time and resources. Two other particular obstacles may also arise: lack of agency policy and lack of response.

Agency policy

Lack of organisational commitment can be a problem. The experience of members of self help groups is that many organisations have yet to adopt policies of support towards self help groups, and to be aware that they can take action to promote them. It is not necessarily always a case of an organisation not appreciating the contribution of groups. Pressure by management to deliver services, limited budgets and the need for crisis work to have priority can all act as a brake, even if staff would like it to be otherwise.

This situation need not necessarily be permanent. There can be changes: change of political control, new government policies and new senior management may alter the atmosphere. Colleagues may be appointed with experience from elsewhere. It may be more a question of biding ones time and spotting opportunities. Any change is likely to be gradual, and perhaps rightly so, for too swift a commitment by an agency to working with self help groups may not be sufficiently grounded to be really effective. It works best when it evolves over time.

Lack of response

Another difficulty may be lack of response, either from colleagues or from members of groups: projects that look good on paper may not work in practice; group secretaries who say they will send literature never put it in the post. Sometimes one cannot know this in advance. Approach new promotional projects as experiments, seeing how they can work, building in time for assessment and then deciding on what might be done in the future. Start with small, manageable projects rather than high profile ones.

See this aspect of working with self help groups in the context of the whole work and priorities of the agency. Promoting self help groups may not be the right way to spend time and it may not be for everyone. Other ways of working with groups may be more appropriate.

Summary

- Consider reasons for promoting self help groups, either as an individual or by an organisation.

- Adopt guidelines and methods relevant to the setting.

- Experiment to see what works and evaluate any projects.

- Be aware of differences between working as a lone champion and when there is agency commitment and policy.

- See it in a broad context of work and priorities and choose whether to take promotion on or not.

10 Listening

Members of self help groups often gather a wealth of knowledge about how to cope with situations and problems, not only through individual experience but through the way that groups allow knowledge to be distilled, shared and passed on. This is more than ordinary 'lay' knowledge and different from folk-lore. Recognising the special knowledge held in groups, and then listening to their members can be very valuable for professionals. There is again the need to be aware of the risks of intrusion and of using the group, unacceptably, for professional ends. On the other hand it is a means of showing that expertise is valued.

Listening to people talking about their group, as opposed to coping with the issue with which it is concerned, is another aspect to this topic. Professionals can learn about the process of helping in self help groups and their variety and get the feel of a particular group. This chapter includes both these topics – the issue or problem and the group – and illustrates how group members' experience can inform and influence professional practice.

Reasons for listening to group members are discussed; a variety of ways to go about it are summarised, and a checklist to help good practice is included. The chapter ends with discussion on the dilemmas and challenges this form of interaction can bring, this time not only for professionals but also for groups.

Why listen?

The term 'listening' is used as a framework for a variety of ways self help groups and professionals can interact. The phrase is not intended to urge professionals to set out to listen, in the sense of putting it in a work plan! Rather, listening, absorbing what is heard and using the information gained can become part of practice at an unconscious level. I don't pose the question 'Why listen' in order to suggest that it is always necessary to formalise what may happen naturally, but instead to help think through more clearly the reasons for doing so and the benefits that can come for both parties. There are four different reasons for listening to people in self help groups:

- To become better informed about a group
- To learn about the issue on which the group is based
- To get feedback on professional care
- To hear views of carers and users, as part of planning services

To become better informed about the group

Most members welcome being asked about their group, how it works and the benefits and difficulties they experience. Listening to people talking about their group, either at meetings or outside them, is a relatively easy and often acceptable way to become better informed about that particular group. It can also help broaden knowledge about self help groups generally.

A professional who knows about how an individual group works may be more comfortable about putting someone in touch with it, and will make the link between the group and possible new members more effectively. They are also more likely to know how to be helpful to the group.

Learning about the issue

The purpose of listening to group members may not be so much to learn about the group, but to learn about the issue on which it is based. There are a number of ways in which this can be done, set out later in this chapter. All of them help the professional to understand more about the illness, problem or issue about which the group is concerned. This may be particularly useful when professional knowledge has not been highly developed and where groups have become experts.

> "Members of one group I know, for people with endometriosis, give very good advice. In a national survey I undertook, most people said that the best information on the condition was from a self help group."   *(Ian, GP)*

The prime purpose of most groups is to help their members directly, but many self help groups would also like professionals to understand more about their situation and ways to cope with it. Listening to people's experience will help professionals become better informed, get an additional perspective than is possible from traditional ways of learning and, as a result, become better at their job.

To get feedback on services

Listening to people may help get feedback on the advice professional agencies · are providing. Diabetic nurses, for example, went regularly to a diabetes group, being quite honest with the group that they came to make professional care more efficient. Nurses felt they needed to know that the advice they were giving in clinics was filtering through and being followed. The group welcomed this, seeing that ultimately people would benefit.

Listening may also be a way to get feedback, not so much about how much notice is being taken of professional advice, but on whether the help being offered is really what people want, and being given in the way they like. The strong emphasis on setting quality standards in many areas of professional care means that listening to people on the receiving end of services may become, not optional, but part of agreed professional practice.

"The social worker should be ready to regard it [the self help group] as a source
of experience from which to learn." *(Adams 1990)*

To hear views about plans for services

Professionals may listen to self help group members to get their views about how services should be planned in the future, either at the field level or as part of a more strategic approach. While planning services at a policy level is not the job of most individual professional workers, field workers may have the opportunity to feed ideas in to planners and may well be involved in detailed service planning.

A physiotherapist, to give an example from day-to-day planning, was in close touch with a group of parents of children with arthritis and regularly used the group as a sounding board for her ideas on how physiotherapy services could be organised. Sometimes she went to the group, other times she asked the group's chairperson to pass her proposals on, aware of how her presence could inhibit discussion. She had also used questionnaires to individuals, but had found it difficult to get real feedback.

"It's a more honest opinion when it's from the group."
(Katherine, Physiotherapist)

Managers and planners will also benefit from listening directly to group members. This broad topic – how users and carers of services can be consulted and heard – is one addressed in much more detail in many other publications. Failing to listen to self help groups could be to ignore a potentially import- ant influence on professional services and the ways they can change for the better.

Action to take

There are a number of ways for professionals to go about this, summarised briefly in Checklist 10.1.

Checklist 10.1   Ways of listening to group members

❑ Attend meetings

❑ Invite members to give talks

❑ Organise special events together

❑ Invite members to attend events run for professionals

❑ Take note of comments on services and plans

❑ Undertake research

❑ Keep in informal contact

Attend meetings

Going to meetings was discussed earlier in this book (Chapter 5, page 45). To recap briefly, some groups make it possible for professionals to attend meet- ings. This might be either through a tradition of open meetings, specially organised meetings or holding meetings with speakers so that it becomes easy for outsiders to be present. Guidelines for visits, as suggested in Checklist 5.4 (page 46) should be followed. And in Chapter 8 on supporting groups, it was suggested that it was important to be clear on what role was being played when visiting a group: adviser, speaker or guest, or a combination of these.

If the prime reason for attending is personal benefit – to learn about the group or the issue – it is particularly important to think about why the visit is being made and what role is being played. Most groups will accept that ben- efit to the professional is a fair reason for attending. They usually want their group to be better known; they would like the issue on which it is based to be better understood, and need services which meet their needs. If the reasons for attending are to achieve one of these, then it is fine to explain this and ask if a visit is possible.

There will be occasions however, when the presence of a professional is an intrusion, perhaps because the issue is so sensitive.

> "A lot of students were coming, because they were doing projects on eating disorders and not explaining this beforehand. We felt 'observed' and uncomfortable, though we welcomed their interest."   *(Kelly, Eating Disorders Group)*

There is another risk. Questions and interest from any outsider may divert the group away from what it really wants to do. It is important to check this with the group, and to be aware of the impact of a non-member's presence. There may be other methods that will work better, rather than going to a regular meeting. If a visit appears to bring real difficulties – and it is important to be sure people are not just being polite about this – it may be better not to attend, but rather to find other ways to go about it.

Invite members to give talks

Taking the initiative and asking group members to come to the professional world may be more appropriate than professionals risking intruding on the self help world. Many groups welcome opportunities to give short talks about their group, or what it is like to be in their situation.

> "Last year, three of us went to speak to psychiatric nurses. I just wish we could get in everywhere."   *(Judith, ME Group)*

On the whole, the professional should take the initiative and make the request, rather than waiting for a group member to ask if they can come. It has proved a discouraging process for group members who have tried unsuccessfully to find their way through the maze of professional structures, and then perhaps to get no response. To recap again, talks by groups can achieve a number of purposes, and when groups and professionals meet each other in this way both parties benefit (Chapter 9). Follow the guidance in Checklist 5.5 (page 47), which summarised how to make talks by group members work well.

Some suggestions in this list may be over-elaborate when there is an easy, close relationship with the group, but are essential if starting from scratch or asking for a real commitment of time and effort. Group members can find giving a talk a daunting experience if they have never done it before, finding proper briefing beforehand reassuring and helpful. Following these guidelines will make it more likely that both group and professionals will find this a helpful experience, beneficial to both.

Organise special events

A short talk may not be enough when professionals would like to develop their knowledge in more depth. The answer may be a specially organised event like a study day.

> "We have very good links with the OT's and went and did a training day. I was asked to nominate so many people to take with me, some carers, some sufferers. Now the Occupational Therapy service is much better informed than it was."
>
> *(Judith, ME Group)*

It seems to work best when the event is planned jointly, the length of the day is decided to fit in with the preference of members of self help groups, numbers are not too large and there is ample time for discussion and questions. It is important to offer to pay travel and any caring costs and, if possible, a fee to the group, just as one would pay a professional expert.

Invite groups to professional events

Some group members, particularly those with experience of giving talks, may be glad to come as speakers at large events designed and run for professionals. Alternatively, where groups have great interest in research on medical conditions, or in knowing more about welfare rights, for example, members may appreciate invitations to attend as participants. The implications here will be first that of cost, for fees charged for professional seminars will be beyond the means of a small self help group, and a bursary scheme will be necessary. It will also be important to make it clear that this is an event designed primarily for professionals, not for groups, so that group members to know what sort of event they will be attending and do not come with any false expectations.

Take note of comments on services and plans

Interaction through events like this give the opportunity to pick up the feelings and experience of people on the receiving end of services informally. It is also possible to take the initiative and approach a group for help when con-sidering changes that might be made in the way services are provided. Many groups are willing to discuss ideas, either when a professional is present or in their absence. It seems to work best when there can be anonymity if needed, when a manageable exercise is being attempted and when the timing is right. A group should be asked its opinion at a time when it can really influence decisions, rather than just before changes are decided. It may be necessary to explain both that their views are important, but just one angle on any changes and that the money available will restrict options. Finally, feed the result of the consultation back to the group.

The initiative to comment on services may not come from the professional but instead the comments may be made by the group itself, unsolicited. This may not always be an easy process but when a group takes the lead it can nevertheless be very useful. A group of parents of children with arthritis, visiting a hospital, were unhappy with what they saw and wrote to the head of department with their suggestions.

> "When we went to visit again, the member of staff in charge had completely changed her organisation to what we had been asking for. It was amazing and she actually thanked us for going along. She wasn't listening to us, we weren't anything really, until we actually went to the top." *(Judith, Parents Group)*

Undertake research

Members of self help groups are very willing to help other people in the same situation as themselves, not only through the activities of the group, but often in contributing to research projects. Research projects have proved to result in greater knowledge about a condition and the needs of people coping with it. They can lead to greater awareness of how services can best be provided, and as a bonus, draw attention to the group.

Even a small research project gives a structured way of listening to group members. An advantage for the professional is access to a willing group of people for their research, if methods allow this. Being invited to take part in a research project will make the group feel valued and members are likely to welcome an opportunity to make a constructive contribution to increasing knowledge about the issue on which their group is based.

Informal contact

None of these methods may be needed if there are easy systems of informal contact between the group and professionals. Regular ways of being in touch may allow the opportunity to try out ideas, get feedback and extend knowledge. A specialist health visitor, for example, who made a point of going regularly to a Down's Syndrome Group "as a visitor" felt she achieved all these. The group was happy with her being there and both saw the relationship as one which benefited both parties.

Informal interaction may not however always be enough, nor give the anonymity which some other methods offer. Check which methods are right, and think whether special efforts are needed, rather than assuming it will happen informally.

Good practice

Use Checklist 10.2 to help think through some of the implications of any action:

Checklist 10.2   Checklist for good practice

❑   Are the planned methods the best for the task in hand?

❑   Can groups choose to co-operate or not?

❑   Might the presence of a professional be an intrusion?

❑   Might involvement by the group mean diverting them from their main purpose?

❑   Will members be out of pocket?

❑   Would a fee be paid to professionals doing the same job?

❑   How can confidentiality, if important to the group, be maintained?

❑   Who should take the initiative?

❑   How representative are the views of the group likely to be?

❑   If not very representative, what other approaches may be needed as well?

❑   How can the group get feedback on the way in which they have influenced practice or improved knowledge?

❑   Who will benefit?

❑   How and by whom will any action be evaluated?

It is now generally agreed that statutory agencies should listen to users and carers and consult voluntary groups. Some of it is included in legislation and policy, the 1990 Community Care Act for example. Many self help groups want to co-operate with requests for their involvement, in principle. In practice, some of the top-down methods used, tight timetables, inaccessible language and the use of formal consultation methods has meant that the special contribution of self help groups has not always been appropriately drawn on.

The methods outlined above have all worked, and have proved possible for both field level workers and groups to manage. The checklist is offered as a way to assess practice and to help professionals become more aware of the possibilities of using informal, low key methods, rather than necessarily adopting formal consultation procedures that may alienate rather than lead to co-operation and mutual benefit.

From time to time, even informal methods of listening need to be assessed, and specific projects or invitations benefit from evaluation. Part of good practice is to monitor and regularly evaluate what has been done, and to ask group members what they think. Only then can good practice evolve and improve.

Dilemmas and challenges

This whole area of practice requires a general openness to other people's opinions. It needs a willingness to learn from people who use professional services as clients, patients or carers. Professionals to whom learning from clients comes naturally will have less difficulty than those who may have to adjust their thinking. But when the two worlds of groups and professionals are interacting, there are likely to be dilemmas and challenges for both worlds:

- A challenge to professional expertise
- The risk of co-option of groups by professionals
- Group members providing only one source of opinions
- A risk of personal pressures on members
- Lack of skills and time

A challenge to professional expertise

A basic tension underlying relationships between self help groups and professionals is likely to be present but not always recognised. The difference between professional knowledge and knowledge gained by experience was discussed in Chapter 4 (page 32). Listening to group members may be a painful experience for some professionals, for groups' comments may appear as a challenge to professional status. This may of course be the case, but it may be just an unfamiliar situation, a process which gets easier through experience and when the value of comments can be seen.

Coping with attacks on colleagues and apparent lack of appreciation of professional services can be more difficult. Disagreement between the group and the professional on how valid information and advice which is being exchanged in a group really is, is a particularly difficult situation to deal with. In this case, the professional should say clearly what their opinion is, speaking directly to the group rather than talking about them to other people. If there is a good relationship with the group this can be quite acceptable. Disagreeing strongly with the group may nevertheless lead to conflict, either personal conflict or between the group and the agency. In this case it may be necessary to accept there will be little chance of co-operation.

Only one source

A dilemma that may arise is that members of groups may be putting forward just one view, when there may well be a number of perspectives. A group of parents of adults with learning difficulties, for example, are likely to have a different point of view from a group of people who themselves have learning difficulties. The professional who feels that the latter are his or her clients may find it difficult to accept the views of a parents' group.

Very occasionally a group may become very committed to a particular course of treatment or approach, to the extent that they are perceived as dogmatic. If their views are in opposition to professional recommendations, there will inevitably be tensions. Enthusiasts for one method are however rare. It is more likely in practice that a group will make available a wide range of information and share a variety of experiences, rather than promote one way of coping.

There are likely to be a number of views and opinions on any question. While a group may put forward a very fair view, it may not be what everyone thinks. Any professional genuinely seeking views on a subject may have to use more than one method or source. Any group putting forward an opinion may have to do so as presenting their view, but recognising that their opinion is not necessarily the ultimate truth.

The risk of co-option and diversion

There are also difficulties for groups. There is a risk for members of groups of co-option and diversion. Self help groups now operate in a climate where, on paper at least, the views of carers and users of services are welcomed and sought. In a wave of enthusiasm for consultation, groups can be 'used' in ways which bring pressure on small volunteer-run organisations. Requests to come to meetings, fill in long questionnaires and take part in committees can lead to the limited energy and time of group members being diverted into meeting professional goals. Just the presence of professionals at group meetings can prevent the process of mutual help taking place. Support and understanding which happens naturally when everyone in the room is affected by the problem is reduced when any outsider is present.

The challenge for the professional is to recognise these possible pressures for groups, to make sure the group has the choice of whether to join in an activity or not and to use an approach and methods which do not intrude on the normal process of the group. It may also mean that the professional has to accept that their request is turned down.

The risk of personal pressures

There is ample evidence that the practice of inviting groups to give talks to professionals can work well and benefit both speaker and audience. There can also be risks and dilemmas for the speaker.

The most effective way for a self-helper to put over a message to a professional audience is for the speaker to tell their story. A personal story explains why a group is needed and how the issue has affected their lives. It can be a very powerful and moving message. It can also have a cost, for telling one's story can be too personal and painful. Recalling a bereavement near the anniversary of someone's death may be too much for a carer or parent for example. Opening oneself up to a professional audience can be intimidating generally.

This can be resolved in a number of ways: many groups only send experienced members as speakers; it can help if they are at some distance from the original problem; speaking to a small audience rather than a large one may be easier. Professionals need to be sensitive to what questions may be appropriate and how to phrase them. The person chairing the session may need to intervene if necessary. In most situations this is not a problem, but has occurred often enough to include it as one of the challenges that may face group members speaking to professionals.

The lack of skills and time

A last point is that professionals may lack skills or simply not have the time, both themes which have come up in previous chapters. While listening skills are likely now to be part of most professionals' training, consultation and research skills are less likely to have been included on a syllabus. Previous jobs may have given little opportunity to develop the special skills which listening to self help groups may require.

Some of the methods suggested here need not so much conscious allocation of large amounts of time, as recognition of the value of what people are saying, and perhaps the need to create the opportunity for them to say it. Some though do need time – and unless this can be deliberately put aside, it may be better not to attempt them. Others may not need many hours spent on a specific project, but depend for their success on having developed a good working relationship with a group. Such a relationship is rarely instant, being more likely to have evolved over time.

On the one hand, listening and responding to what is heard should become a naturally integrated part of good professional practice; on the other, imposition on a small voluntary group must be avoided. If both groups and professionals share the same agenda, then listening to self help groups can work well for both.

Summary

- Think why professionals might want to listen to members of self help groups.

- Adopt methods which are right for both parties.

- Assess and evaluate what is done, asking groups what they think and make changes where needed.

- Be aware of difficulties and challenges, for both group members and professionals.

Section three

Common threads

11 Matching the approach

One theme of this book is that there is no one set procedure, no approved protocol to follow when professionals are working with self help groups. On the other hand, as readers will have seen from the previous five chapters, there is proven good practice on which to draw and guidelines for action which should be used as the basis of professionals' work.

There is also another theme: match the approach with the situation. Matching should be considered as part of good practice. People with some experience in this field will already appreciate the need for variety in how they work with self help groups, having been able to use their experience, distill it and know what seems to work best in different situations. In this chapter on matching the approach, I identify a number of variables that are likely to influence practice. The different questions discussed are, first, the nature of the issue on which the group is based. How highly structured the group is and how long it is likely to last are covered, followed by a look at social factors, including the needs of people from black and ethnic minorities. The final topic covered is the need to take into account the individuals concerned and the outlook and policies of both the agency and the particular professional.

Fig 11.1 summarises how these variables, presented horizontally, can cut across the suggested five areas of practice dealt with in the previous chapters, listed vertically. The five variables interweave with and often affect how work will be carried out.

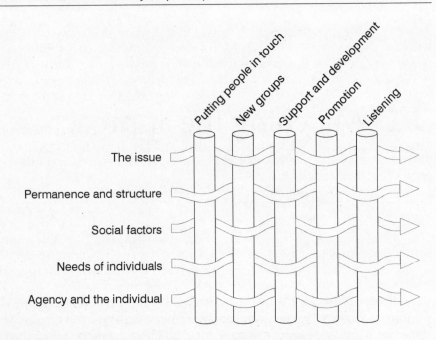

Figure 11.1 Issues cutting across areas of good practice

The nature of the issue

Self help groups form around a very wide range of issues, conditions and problems. While there are values common to most self help groups, the nature of the issue on which they are based often leads to differences in how they work in practice. Putting them in broad categories can help see some of these distinctions. I draw here not only on the experience of professionals and groups in the field, but also on the recent work of Mai Wann on self help groups and public policy *(Wann 1995)*. She distinguishes between six different categories, to which I have added a seventh:

- Physical illness
- Disability
- Mental health and well being
- Addiction
- Carers groups
- Social issues
- Generalist support groups

There are overlaps between these categories and variations between groups within a category, but having some idea of these divisions will be helpful. It may be necessary to work differently according to the type of group. It may also be best to concentrate learning about self help groups on a particular type of group, so developing close links with one type of group and looser links with others.

Physical illness groups   There are large numbers of groups based on physical illness, formed around both chronic and life threatening conditions. Individuals may join to break their isolation, share their worries and find out more about their condition.

Many groups focus on coping strategies. Their members can become very expert in knowing how to live with an illness, as individuals and as a group holding a body of knowledge. The implications of working with this type of group will include the need to recognise their expertise and how this affects the professional role. Professionals may also need to be aware that people often prefer to join a very specific group, rather than one based on general health issues.

Disability groups   Disabilities may be a direct result of illness or treatment, so there can be overlaps between these two types. The growing demand for control over their own lives is an important theme in groups run by disabled people. The social model of disability sees the problem in society rather than in people with disabilities and disabled people are increasingly challenging the ethos of national charities still based on a tradition of benevolence rather than empowerment. One may also see another thread among some disability groups: the need for social activities to help deal with problems of isolation, particularly among older disabled people. This is often a reason for starting a group.

Professionals working with disability groups will need to be aware of this range of perspectives and the potential challenge to their role too, a challenge which is likely to grow.

Mental health and well being   This very broad category, suggests Wann, covers a wide range of activities, from prevention of mental illness to dealing with phobias and life crises such as bereavement. Some groups have general names, to avoid stigma. Others deliberately use the name of an illness as part of the process of owning and coping with their situation.

One issue arising in this range of groups is the degree of support that may be needed from professionals. It may be, as Wann argues, that groups whose members have a history of psychiatric problems have a greater need for a facilitator to take on the backbone role outlined in Chapter 7. The mental health user movement would reject this approach and groups based on issues such as bereavement may well prefer very little intervention in their work. No one clear role arises for the professional with this very broad range of groups.

Groups concerned with an addiction   This category includes Alcoholics Anonymous and other groups based on the 12 Step principles developed by AA. 12 Step groups include in their traditions a principle of being self-supporting, meaning that offers of help from outside will be turned down. Many 12 step groups have systems of open meetings, so making it simpler to visit and learn from than from some other groups.

Drug users groups come in this category, which also covers groups for people dependent on or coming off tranquillisers. A complex factor for professionals working with tranquilliser groups is that people have normally only become dependent because of prescribing practices by doctors, and so group members are often very angry about the professional treatment they have received.

In this field people may be members of a group for a long time. This is not dependence in a negative sense, but rather a matter of choosing long-term membership, finding this helps cope with life. An issue often raised by professionals is that self help groups can make people dependent on groups. Professionals may rather need to see that people's choice to stay a member of a group for a long time is one to be accepted, not criticised.

Carers groups   Carers groups may be generalist, for anyone caring for someone who is frail, disabled or severely ill, or specific such as the Alzheimer's Disease Society. There has been a substantial growth of such groups in the last decade and they have contributed to major changes in social policy.

Professionals who care about a whole family need to be well informed about carers groups as well as groups formed to meet the needs of people directly affected by a condition. The professional role may well include the need for the carer to be given the option to attend a group, as much as the person who is the professional's client or patient. There may too be a need to accept a conflict of interest, for the concern of carers groups can be in opposition to the perspective of users' groups. Occasionally, professionals may find themselves presented with dilemmas of which to support.

Social issues   Among those who form self help groups in this category are lone parents, victims of domestic violence, families of offenders and survivors of sexual abuse, of which there are increasing numbers of groups. This category of groups may be particularly changeable, affected by social attitudes and conditions and by new issues becoming visible.

Confidentiality and privacy will be very important in most groups based on social issues, meaning that a particularly sensitive approach by professionals will be needed. Where the issue is becoming more accepted, single parenthood for example, public support by professionals is seen by groups as an endorsement of their work and there may be less need for privacy.

Generalist support groups Groups which are much less specific in their remit have similar aims of mutual support and sharing information to more specific groups, but cover a broad area of interest: a women's health group for example, a group about health for elderly people or a support group attached to a church, mosque or temple.

A professional employed as a community worker or working in a particular neighbourhood will be most interested in supporting groups like these. Any professional, nevertheless, should be aware that such groups exist and may be very useful. People who prefer not to take what can be a major step of taking on a label of a particular illness or situation may be happy to go to a general support group.

See this section as a snapshot. A brief summary can only pick out some characteristics of these different categories of groups and variations within groupings may be so great that this sketch may prove to be too rough a tool. It is offered more as a checklist, to help assess working practice and to see where a professional may need to concentrate learning and effort. This categorisation will also help make it clearer as to why an approach can be successful in one area, but not transfer when working with a very different category of self help group.

Degree of permanence and structure

As well as the type of group, professional practice will be influenced by the extent to which a group is likely to be permanent and the degree of structure in its organisation. Some groups last only a short time, others for decades. Some, usually highly structured, are part of national organisations. Key members in groups can affect both how permanent and how structured a group is.

Length of life

Well-known, long-standing groups with a certain status in a community can be easier for professionals to relate to than short-term, impermanent and often informal groups. Both are legitimate ways of organising but working methods may vary considerably with one type or the other.

One example of how professional practice can vary concerns putting people in touch with groups. It will be generally agreed that giving outdated information is best avoided but it will be necessary to check that the group is still in existence more often when the group is likely to have a limited life. The difficulty of locating short-term groups may be overcome by using more general contact points. A direct search for a group may be less appropriate than using sources of information which may hold details about a particular set of groups. An organisation concerned with lone parents for example, will be in touch with a wide range of single parent groups. A community centre will be familiar with a range of local groups in the neighbourhood.

Links with national organisations

Different approaches may be needed for groups affiliated to national organisations and for 'lone' groups. Lone groups may particularly value support. A group may either be independent by choice or through lack of any other option, for there may be no appropriate national organisation. In either case, there may well be a role for the professional in helping members of lone groups develop structures and groundrules.

Other groups have links with national organisations concerned with the same issue on which they are based. This can give them more stability and visibility, making it easier for the professional to get to know them. If a group is operating as a branch of a nationally known organisation a professional may feel more confident about a group, although this should not be seen as a guarantee for reliability.

Key individuals

Permanence and structure may not depend on a link with a national organisation but rather on a key individual. Even in groups which are technically founded on princples of member involvement and shared decision making, this is often the reality. One implication of this is that a group may come to an abrupt end if the person concerned withdraws, becomes too ill or even dies.

There may be a contribution a professional can make as part of a supportive role. This could be supporting a key individual, and sustaining them until a new group has a broader base of organisation. It could be through helping them develop ways of involving new members and creating traditions of newcomers gradually contributing to the group. Or professionals may have an opportunity to help someone move to a new role, rather than holding a grip on a group.

Some founders can hold a grip to the extent of dominating the group, being too authoritative and paternalistic. Any key member may keep too firm a control, resulting in stifling growth and sometimes the group ending. Avoiding this happening in the first place is the best approach, for once control is established, an outsider cannot easily alter a situation. Professionals will need to be realistic about the limits to their intervention.

A founder is not always a constraint. The founder member is as often a positive force in a group, an enormous strength, and making it more effective than one with a more transient membership. The professional role is not necessarily one of helping someone to move on but to support them in their role.

Social factors

We come now to a range of issues, grouped as social factors which can influence how groups run, who they might suit and the form of relationships professionals might have with them. The issues covered are:

- Social class
- Ethnic background
- Age
- Gender
- Geographical location

All these are complex issues, raised as subjects needing thought rather than offering firm conclusions and solutions. Much more research is needed before real conclusions can be reached and proper strategies established.

Social class   It may be helpful to see a self help group on a point on a continuum as far as social class and income is concerned. Visualise a line with middle class at one end and working class at the other and imagine how a group would be located on it. At either end of the continuum could be a clustering of members from a particular social background or there could be a real mix of class and social backgrounds. If there is a mix, class then would not be so much of an issue for the concern which had brought everyone together would be a strong uniting force. In many groups, background and job recede and members are united by their common interest and social class is not always a point to consider.

If, though, the clustering of members at either end of the class continuum is a strong characteristic of a group, then this will be part of professional knowledge of a group and will need to be an issue taken account of when working with them. For example, there may be a greater need to take time to introduce a new member to the group. Sometimes it may be possible to help a group get over what can be a limit on its work. When choosing a venue for meetings, for example, a professional may be able to draw attention to the value of a neutral meeting place, and help a group consider that, balancing it out with any advantages of meeting in people's homes. Many groups meet in neutral surroundings to enable people from any social background to feel comfortable about attending.

Ethnicity   It is common for issue based self help groups to have a largely white membership, though this is not universal. Some groups have a mix of people from a variety of ethnic backgrounds and in the same way as class recedes as an issue, so can ethnicity. It is an issue needing much more consideration, though some authors have begun to address it *(Tavistock Institute of Human Relations 1989, Agbalaya 1993).*

There is some evidence of black people having been made feel less than welcome in largely white groups and professionals may need to help a group be aware of equal opportunities practices though this may be an unfamiliar term to many group members. A group may say they are open to all; professionals may have a role to play in helping this be put into practice. They may be able to ask questions, for example, to help create awareness of the issue. They may be able to introduce black members to the group more systematically and help create a balance in membership.

Groups are not always ethnically mixed for they may be formed not only about an issue but specifically for people from one particular background. A divorced Asian women's group is likely to be more effective in meeting Asian women's needs than a divorced women's group for all women. Black carers groups give the opportunity for members to socialise, share recipes and discuss issues relating to the black community or home background which they might feel constrained to mention in a predominantly white group *(Fielding 1990).* Other groups form around conditions specific to ethnic minorities, such as sickle cell anaemia. People for whom English is not their first language may prefer a group where their first language is spoken. The traditions of some cultures may mean that a group only for men or only for women is needed.

Supporting the growth of such groups can be another professional role, especially for professionals from the same background. Sometimes the professional role may be to help a wider group understand the need for specific black groups to form within, or outside the main organisation. To meet people's needs for support a professional may also need to get access to information about groups far wider than the groups which form the main thrust of this book. For self help and mutual aid are not the preserve of issue specific self help groups. People from ethnic minorities may prefer support in a more general setting such as a church, temple or through adult education or social activities, in groups which are informal and loosely structured.

Age   Many groups based on an issue cover a range of ages, though in some cases the nature of the issue naturally influences who may be interested in joining. Where this is not so, it may be useful to check the age range a group covers, and to think whether any work undertaken will be influenced by the age range a group covers.

Specific groups are sometimes formed: a young widowed group, for example, began from the experience of younger widowed women who found their needs were not met within a broader widows group. There may be a role in supporting people who find themselves in this sort of situation, for sometimes they can feel disloyal to the original group and have difficulty in voicing their particular needs. It may also be necessary to check the age range of a group before putting someone in touch with it. With breast cancer, for example, the experience and outlook of younger women with breast cancer may be very different from women in their sixties. Parents groups may concentrate on a specific age range of children. Where there is only one group, and so no choice, a new member can sometimes be linked with an individual member of a similar age before they join the group which will help them feel they belong.

Gender   Sharing the same situation is not always enough: people often need to be with people who face the same situation but also in the same context. This has been particularly marked with women. While it is common to find groups specifically for women, men are beginning to recognise the need to be together on their own and some men's groups are forming too. Cultural traditions may affect membership of groups as well, for religious or community customs may be for groups to be single-sex.

Decisions to limit membership to men or to women should be accepted as a choice that may be taken by a group, but if it happens casually it can make people feel shut out, rather than be a strength. A bereaved parents group for example, with a tradition for women to attend and take the lead, but not publicised as being only for women, will be unlikely to feel open to men. As with age, a professional may need to find out the balance of men and women in a group. If this seems to have the effect of excluding some people, it may be possible to raise this and help a group discuss how to deal with the issue; groups may simply not be aware of how an imbalance in gender can prevent some people from getting much-needed support.

Geographical area   Interwoven with the issues of class and ethnic background is the question of geographical location: whether the group is urban or rural and, in a city, from what neighbourhood it largely draws its membership.

There will be little choice for people in areas where there are few self help groups, but in districts where there are many of them, groups based on neighbourhood as well as issue allow choice and ease of access. Carers groups, for example, have found this an appropriate way to organise. A woman starting a group for people with a visual impairment had a vision of a network of local groups in a city rather than one centralised group, a vision now realised. Organising on a neighbourhood basis can ease transport problems, make groups more accessible, save time and make contact between members outside group meetings much easier. Professionals helping new groups start can help initiators be aware of such advantages and there may also be opportunities for professionals to help solve problems of transport, a major problem in rural areas. Practical backup by a professional agency may be essential for groups in scattered communities *(Hills et al. 1988)*.

A local group may be quite the wrong place for individuals who do not want to meet people they know already. For reasons of confidentiality, some people prefer to go to a group away from their home, to be able to be anonymous. Professionals may need to know how to get information about groups out of their area to help meet this need.

The needs of individuals

We move on now from social factors to the needs of individuals. Some professional contact with individuals will be brief and transient; patients coming to a hospital Accident and Emergency Department, for example. In this case, it will be more important to have a standard system for putting people in touch with groups than trying to tailor it to the needs of an individual.

Many professsionals however have long-term contact with clients or patients, giving the opportunity to tailor the way people are put in touch with a group and for the method used to fit people's needs as individuals. The system suggested for putting people in touch with a group in Chapter 5 was that everyone should get to know the group existed. Just how they might be put in touch or introduced to the group can be done to suit the individual concerned. Checklist 11.1 summarises how putting people in touch can be done in a variety of ways, which allow an individualised approach but enable everyone to have access to information about a group.

Checklist 11.1　Ways professionals can link people with groups

❑　Display a poster

❑　Tell the person the group exists

❑　Give them details of meetings and the contact person

❑　Weigh up together the pros and cons of going

❑　Invite group members to meet people currently using the service

❑　Ring the group to make an introduction

❑　Go with the individual to the first meeting

The list begins with low-key ways of linking, when the professional has little involvement and ends with a high degree of professional involvement. Low or high intervention is not right or wrong, the question is much more what is right for the person concerned and of being aware of the variety of different methods which can be appropriate. Other ways of working with self help groups – helping new groups and supporting established groups – will also be influenced by the individuals concerned and their needs.

Agency policies and individual outlooks

The final issues considered in this chapter are the organisation and its outlook and policies and the individual professional: first, the organisation.

Agency policies and experience

How people work with self help groups and how important it is in their work may well depend on the organisation for which they work. The situation will be very different working in an agency where groups' contribution is neither appreciated nor visible, to one where their work is endorsed, welcomed and supported by policies and established practice. Checklist 11.2 offers a way of seeing where an agency might be on a scale of interest. If most of these points would get a tick, then one would expect the level of interest to be high, and vice versa.

Checklist 11.2   Organisations and self help groups

❑ Lay, voluntary contributions to care generally valued

❑ Public endorsement by management

❑ Publicity about self help groups displayed

❑ Use of premises for meetings

❑ Group members visit offices, wards and departments

❑ Groups listed in agency handbooks and leaflets

❑ Subject included in induction and in-service training

❑ Time-off-in-lieu given for staff attending evening meetings

❑ Students undertake projects with self help groups

❑ Grants and practical support available

Working in an agency which scores high on many of these factors will mean that it will be much easier for individual professionals to incorporate working with self help groups into their day-to-day work. They are more likely to be able to learn from experienced colleagues and share some of the difficulties and challenges with people who have also experienced them.

Working in a place where few or none of the activities summarised above take place, and where the values and attitudes of most of the staff make it unlikely that they would be part of normal practice, will mean that a professional may well be working in isolation. Working with self help groups will then be a much more difficult task.

The individual professional

The last point to be considered is the way in which one works may be affected by personal experience. Some professionals are themselves members of a group, or have been in the past. If this has been a helpful experience, it is likely that work with self help groups will be a comfortable part of a professional job, with understanding of the advantages and difficulties that belonging to a group may bring. Other professionals may not have been a group member, but may instinctively be at ease working in this way.

Some professionals have direct experience of the situation with which a group is concerned, which may or may not make them more interested in a group. Anecdotes from groups suggest that while there can be greater interest than there might have been, other professionals seem to avoid a group if they have the same problem themselves.

If professionals join a group as a member, to get personal support, then another question arises. Personal experience of a situation will mean that a professional attending a group has to decide whether they are there as a member – or as a professional. This has to be made clear to other members of the group for it can be confusing for everyone to play both roles at once.

Potential clash

To recap, professionals can work with self help groups in all five ways summarised in Fig 11.1. The five areas of practice may have to be tempered, however, by the issues which are likely to be present as well. There may be choices to make if both these dimensions are taken on board.

Summary

- The nature of the issue on which a group is based can affect how it works and the type of relationship with professionals.

- Long-term groups may be easier to relate to than short-term groups, which may require a different approach.

- Groups are affected by how highly structured they are and the extent to which they have one or more leading members.

- A range of social factors influence both groups and the nature of their relationship with professionals.

- The needs of individuals have to be taken into account and methods adopted to meet those needs.

- The characteristics of an agency and of an individual professional will influence the relationship.

12 No magic wand

Both self help groups and professionals can assume that it is easy to work together, but the two worlds – that of self help groups and that of professionals – are very different. Both can over-idealise the relationship, neither seeing the whole picture nor being aware of traditions and undercurrents. Even if there is a close working relationship, the two worlds may have dissimilar expectations and, almost built into the relationship, there are likely to be barriers and constraints.

The relationship of self help groups and professionals should be set against the context of other, broader issues, such as racism, sexism and other prejudices and discrimination in society. These issues are not explored here, but it should be acknowledged that professionals and self-helpers are operating in a society where power is held and exerted by some sections of society more than others; this, too, may influence relationships. Once one accepts the likelihood of barriers and constraints, then it becomes possible to be realistic about the time and effort, on both sides, that may be needed before there can be fruitful working relationships. A member of a carers group for relatives of people with Alzheimer's Disease, committed to working with professionals in the health and social services, saw the picture clearly: "There's no magic wand to wave to make sure relationships work well," said Martin, "You've got to work at it."

This chapter draws together themes of dilemmas, difficulties and tensions running through this book. The whole issue of using a community development, enabling approach in a world where the delivery of services takes precedence will first be raised. Four broad constraints, all apparent in most areas of working with self help groups are identified and discussed: traditions of professional authority and power; conflicts of interest; the nature of self help groups; and the lack of agreed good practice.

141

Community development in a service delivery world

Enabling, valuing, empowering and acknowledging the importance of self determination are all elements of a community development approach. It is not necessary to be a community worker to work in this way, and many professionals will be used to this approach when working with individuals. A community development approach underlies much of the guidance offered in the five chapters in Section two.

In contrast, most health and social service professionals are working in a culture which is based on specific service delivery. Increasingly, contracts which require reports on the quantity of work carried out form the basis of professional care. There are bound to be difficulties and clashes if requirements of employers, government, funders and purchasers do not include room to adopt an enabling approach, which needs a long-term investment of time before results can be seen. In Area Social Services Departments in particular, crisis intervention takes precedence over a longer-term, arguably more preventative approach.

As well as this general issue of potential tension, four other themes appear in most areas of good practice, each now looked at in some detail:

- Traditions of professional authority and knowledge
- Conflicts of interest
- The unpredictable nature of self help groups
- Lack of agreed good practice

Traditions of professional authority and knowledge

Traditions of professional authority and knowledge can be looked at from both a professional perspective and from the point of view of the lay world of self help groups, whose members may actually endorse this power.

Professional authority

Built in to all professions are commitment and traditions, such as undertaking training, staying well informed and operating to agreed professional standards. These traditions are essential when a professional is operating in their own arena and form in part the basis of professional authority. Once professionals are working in the self help world, however, the whole question of authority needs to be re-assessed. The knowledge professionals hold will now be set alongside knowledge self-helpers have gained through experience.

Authority also comes from a position held in an organisation or society. Professional status can be a barrier to productive working relationships with self help groups and, as a number of illustrations have portrayed, inappropriate exercise of professional power can sometimes prevent their successful development. Even professionals aware of this risk and attempting to work in a non-authoritative way may not be sufficiently aware of how their position can inhibit what they are attempting to do.

Lay endorsement

The reason for any imbalance of power is not only professional status. To some extent, this aspect of the relationship is endorsed by the individual lay person. As recipients of professional care, we all want the person concerned with our needs to be knowledgeable and skilled. We become dependent on their help, at least for a time, and we are often very grateful for their services. To switch to a situation where the self-helper is in charge and is an expert is a difficult step for many people.

People currently receiving professional help have a particular situation to deal with. It may not always be acknowledged that self-helpers can be very nervous of working with people in authority, as members of self help groups, if they have other personal relationships with professionals as clients or patients, or as carers. They may find it difficult to question professional practice towards their group when, as individuals, they are dependent on professionals' direct help and the control they have over access to other resources.

Lay confidence

Considering another country where self help groups are well developed may be helpful. Compared to the United States, where people tend to be much more assertive about their needs and rights, people in Britain tend to have inbuilt attitudes of respect for professional status and to find it difficult to assert their own views.

The experience of being a member of a self help group often leads to greater confidence and assertiveness. The traditional professional world, particularly in medicine, may either find this very difficult to cope with, or reject it as being dogmatism or dedication to a cause. A majority of group members are women; increased assertiveness of women and their feelings about their health needs has led to major changes in health care. Increasingly, physically disabled people and survivors of mental health services are voicing their needs and the approach they want professionals to take. It may well be that people in younger generations, growing up in this culture, will find it easier to work co-operatively with professionals, rather than putting them on a pedestal, which many people in older age groups have tended to do.

On the surface, both self-helpers and many professionals may want and try to operate to principles of self determination, acknowledgement of the value of lay knowledge and ownership of groups by their members. Underneath, people in both worlds may find it difficult to change or challenge any imbalance of power. The first step is recognition. Acknowledging the existence of the barrier of traditions of professional authority and knowledge is necessary for both parties in the relationship. Then one may decide what steps to take, if any, to deal with it.

Conflicts of interest

When groups criticise or comment on professional practice an obvious conflict of interest between the two worlds of self help groups and professionals may arise. Issues raised by self-helpers about professional care may be in direct opposition to professional views, though experience suggest that this is far from being widespread. It is more likely that comments will be helpful. Nonetheless, there will be tensions when groups are campaigning for major changes where these are not endorsed by influential professionals.

There may be conflicts of interests too when people are unhappy with the treatment they are receiving as individuals. As members of groups, this can mean that working relationships with professionals are difficult.

Less obvious are a number of other potential conflicts of interest which we now examine. The good of the client or patient, as defined by the professional, against a principle of people being able to make decisions for themselves is one. The difficulty of a commitment to service users and meeting their needs on the one hand, and those of their families and carers on the other, is another. There can also be a conflict of interest between concern to protect vulnerable people from unnecessary distress and preventing other people having access to help.

The good of the client

Putting people in touch with groups is the area particularly likely to be influenced by questions raised by professionals concerned first with the good of the client or patient. Concern to match help with the individual's needs, as perceived by the professional, may be a traditional and important part of professional practice. At what stage, however, does this become paternalism?

As illustrated in Chapter 5, there are differing views on giving information selectively and universal practice of putting people in touch, with self-helpers strongly opting for everyone being told. The built-in tension here is not always recognised – by either side.

There may be particular issues to be faced when people are suffering from a degenerative illness. Professionals are known to have held back information about groups for people with, for example, multiple sclerosis, on the basis that people will feel worse if they see people worse than themselves. Self-helpers would argue that if people have the chance to discuss such issues before and while going to such groups, it is not a major problem. They point out that parents of children attending toy libraries, people sitting in waiting areas for outpatients clinics and so on are likely to see others in worse situations than their own. Issues about timing, when is the best time to tell people about groups, and supporting them if needed should be addressed, but there is also a question of whether professionals can err towards being over-protective and controlling.

Service user's needs v. carers and families

In many areas of work professionals try to look at the needs of the whole family. In some situations, nonetheless, it is likely that the needs of the person directly using a professional service are put first, with implications for support for self help groups. Current professional practice in the field of learning difficulties for example, means that a professional is likely to work with their client to help them become as independent as possible. It may be difficult simultaneously to support a group of their parents who appear to be working to meet their own needs as parents, from a more traditional approach. An agency concerned with people dependent on drugs may not be able to give attention to the very different needs of their families and friends, because of the need for confidentiality.

The needs of carers generally have increasingly been recognised. The conflict of interest this can bring for professionals working with self help groups may not always be obvious.

A concern to protect v. giving access to services

A third conflict of interest will arise when the needs of certain groups of people, as seen by the professional, are put before giving others access to services. This question came up in the discussion on posters in Chapter 6 (page 59). Efforts to promote and publicise self help groups are likely to include making difficult issues visible. There is some evidence that professionals have declined to publicise some groups on the grounds that users of services will find a reminder of the existence of the problems they address distressing. Ensuring people avoid unnecessary distress could be seen as good professional practice – or, again, as being protective. People are bound to be exposed to difficult issues in their everyday lives and through the media.

Occasionally the question may be to protect a group, particularly if it is new and vulnerable, or to risk putting someone in touch with it who may cause real difficulties to their members. Professionals may face the dilemma of whether to tell someone about a group, when they can see that person could threaten a group's structure or hold back information that could help the individual.

To sum up, a range of conflicts of interest may underlie relationships, some overt but some concealed. There are many dilemmas here for professionals and a need to consider how to resolve potential conflicts of interest, if indeed this is possible. There may be no easy answer.

The nature of self help groups

Self help groups are difficult groups to run. A simple idea in theory – people in the same situation getting together for mutual support – in practice they are far from simple and their unpredictability can make it difficult for professionals to work effectively with them. Four particular types of difficulties often arise when people are starting and running self help groups, all of which professionals need to be aware of:

- Lack of experience
- Problems normally experienced in any small, volunteer-run groups
- Limits arising from the issue on which the group is based
- Lack of knowledge and support to help groups learn how to work with professionals

Lack of experience

People who form self help groups often feel drawn to do so through experiencing some trauma in their lives and having a strong desire to overcome isolation. They have rarely, as they often say, done anything like this before. People learn on the job. Sometimes help is forthcoming from other groups, from national organisations and from local development agencies but this is not universally available and many groups work in the dark. Some initiators may be unaware of even simple traditions like the need for confidentiality and groundrules on how meetings are run.

Small-group problems

Most small groups, not just self help groups, face problems at some time. These may arise from strong personalities, from founders holding on to positions too long or from strong friendship bonds resulting in newcomers feeling unwelcome. Some of these issues are likely to be resolved as a group settles down but others may prove more difficult.

The central issue

The issue on which the group is based often results in constraints on the group. Lack of mobility, limited energy and the demands that the caring role places on members are examples of difficulties many people in groups face. Awareness of these constraints and how some of them can be addressed can lead to them being seen, and accepted, as limits within which a group works. Professionals unaware of the nature of self help groups can have expectations that they will run like other voluntary groups without such limits, and then make inappropriate requests or arrangements.

The issue can mean, also, that a group only meets for a limited time. It may be that members feel that they have achieved what they wanted by meeting together and decide to end the group, often with a sense of achievement. The true story of the infertility support group which came to an end when all its members had babies is an example.

It is not always quite as clearcut. There can be situations where people gain strength from the group and move on to involvement with the wider community and to getting on with their own lives. This can be fine for them, but unless the group has a tradition of members taking on jobs in turn, a small core of people who choose not to leave may be left doing all the work. In this case, success for individuals may mean a dwindling group of longstanding members, who are not sure whether to continue or not and perhaps become a little detached from the needs of new members.

Professionals wanting to work with self help groups will find it easier if they become aware of these and other common situations which result from the issue on which the group is based. Sometimes their support may resolve some of these difficulties. If, however, the stimulus to the group being formed is anger about professional care or rejection of its approach, then the situation is likely to be more challenging. Over time and with good channels of communication, barriers can be overcome, but this may not be the case in all situations. Professionals need to recognise that where there is little overlap between the two worlds, and very different goals for self-helpers and the professional world, co-operation may be unrealistic.

Limited knowledge of group/professional relationships

While longstanding members of groups may become very informed and aware of how they can best work with the professional world, this is not always the case. Some national organisations make guidelines available, and if some members of a group are themselves professionals, they can bridge the gap. It is more likely though that groups will have limited knowledge about the professional world and be unaware of the often complex issues underlying the relationships between the two. Nor will they be familiar with structures and communication systems in professional agencies.

'Good Links', a publication written for group members suggests guidelines for good working relationships from the self-helper's point of view *(Wilson 1994a)*, but knowledge about group/professional relationships from the self-helper's perspective is still at an early stage. Members, like many professionals, may have competence, goodwill and enthusiasm but not had the chance to learn about how best to deal with some of the challenges. Professionals supporting self help groups can often help by providing information and giving access to professional systems of communication, which may get over some of these problems.

A matter of choice

Members of self help groups have to make choices, for they face competing demands within the broad limits of time they can make available for their group. Groups may simply choose not to spend their limited time, energy and resources on working with professionals. They may decide to concentrate on simple activities, preferring to be more inward looking to their own needs, rather than outward looking to the needs of others. Professionals need to be aware of the need for choice and to recognise the risk of diverting limited resources away from the main activity of a group by too many requests for liaison and co-operation.

To sum up, the nature of self help groups may act as a further constraint on the development of good working relationships with professionals. Good practice is best based on a sense of reality of how they work, rather than on idealised or inaccurate expectations. Group members want professionals to accept them as they are.

Lack of agreed good practice

Finally, we turn to the question of the lack of consensus in the professional world on what makes for good practice in working relationships between self help groups and professionals. Without some consensus on broad principles, it is difficult to include the topic in professional training but no professional bodies have yet produced guidelines, let alone training material. Five topics are explored:

- The impact and limits of lone pioneers
- Lack of protocols
- Learning on the job
- Self-helpers' expectation of professional knowledge
- Lack of investment in intermediaries

Lone pioneers

Vivid examples in this book show that some people working in the health and social services, across a variety of professions, are expert in working with self help groups. They are more likely to be lone pioneers, the only person in their organisation working in this way, rather than a whole team of people becoming proficient in the area. While this may be one way that a new area of expertise develops, it nonetheless has its limits.

People working in this way can feel isolated and under pressure and without support themselves do not necessarily continue to support self help groups. They may be working in effect as volunteers, meaning if they leave the post there will be no commitment from an employer that the same investment of time will be made by a successor. Work by lone pioneers does not have the same status as an approach adopted by the organisation as a whole.

Lack of protocols

It is unlikely that working with self help groups will need the same precise protocols that say child protection work by social workers or lifting techniques for nurses require. The establishment of protocols can, though, lead to greater status and to systematic work by an agency, rather than an erratic dependence on the skill and commitment of a few individuals. Once there has been more thought given to what is good practice in specific settings, then the adoption of guidelines, at least, may overcome some of these constraints.

Learning on the job

Few professionals have the opportunity to learn about working with self help groups in pre-professional training or through in-service training. As a result, most professionals who have gained expertise in this area have learnt it as they went along. If they work in an agency with established traditions of working with self help groups, this may help, but is still unlikely to lead to adoption of agreed principles and standards. Learning on the job should complement other learning techniques, not be the single method of learning, but to date that would seem to be the only way most professionals learn.

Expectation of knowledge

An additional problem may arise when self-helpers assume that professionals do get training in this area, members expecting that there is expertise and knowledge which does not in fact exist. A qualification in a particular profession does not necessarily result in being able to work effectively with self help groups. Where the group makes an assumption that this is the case, there may be frustrations and tensions, and difficulties being attributed by the group to prejudice and power, when in fact the professional simply has not had the opportunity to learn.

Lack of investment in intermediaries

Finally, lack of investment in infrastructures holds back the development of good relationships. A number of health authorities, social service departments and NHS Trusts, for example, Southern Derbyshire *(Haggard 1993)*, see that funding an intermediary body helps the process. Health and social services authorities which invest money in local self help centres and workers, often based in a local Council for Voluntary Service, find that their work saves professional time and gives access to expertise. Authorities see it not just as a funding matter but as an endorsement of an approach which their staff may otherwise consider risky.

Funding local, generalist self help development services is generally felt to be an effective way of making self help group/professional relationships develop and thrive *(Wann 1995)*. In other areas of professional work, it is accepted that resource centres, advisers and information databases are needed and are good investments. Without this general recognition and allocation of resources in the field of self help activity, it is unlikely that relationships will be fully effective.

In all, there is not yet consensus on good practice; there is not investment in training and infrastructures; and there is not yet the recognition of the time needed to make relationships between self help groups and professionals work. As the carer said, there is no magic wand. While some constraints can be overcome, others need to be acknowledged and lived with as part of the relationship.

Summary

- An enabling, empowering approach may be incompatible with a service delivery culture.

- Traditions and expectations of professional power and authority can act as a constraint.

- Conflicts of interest, in many forms, need recognised.

- The nature of self help groups themselves may make the development of relationships difficult, for both sides.

- Groups may simply choose to use their limited time in other ways than working with professionals.

- Lack of consensus and adoption of good practice acts as a constraint on good working relationships.

- Lack of investment in infrastructures limits what can be achieved.

13 Growth for both

In this final chapter the theme of mutual benefit is explored but first the key competencies – the areas of skill and knowledge that a professional who is serious about working with self help groups should hold – are summarised. A competent professional:

- Understands the value of self help groups
- Respects their autonomy and the need for confidentiality
- Knows a little can go a long way
- Creates opportunities for interaction
- Builds working with self help groups into individual work and organisational systems
- Sees how everyone can benefit when relationships work well

The book ends by exploring the theme of mutual benefit. Aiming for both halves to benefit provides a firm foundation for any relationship. Honest give-and-take and appreciation of the skills and experience of both parties make any joint venture much more likely to work. Working relationships between self help groups and professionals which start from this perspective and see the likelihood of mutual benefit will lead to growth for them both.

Understanding the value

A competent professional understands and values the strengths of self help groups but also appreciates their boundaries, appreciating groups as they are and want to be, not expecting them to act as if they were other forms of organisation. Professional care also has its limits: professionals working with self help groups should be aware, as well, of the limits to results a professional can achieve, not necessarily because of lack of resources or skills, but simply because they are a professional, working in a professional setting. The competent professional values the diversity of help from the two worlds.

If there are difficulties, they are prepared to ride out the storms and to see the ultimate value of creative tension, even if there are painful periods and challenges to authority. This does not mean self help groups are always right, and there may be sticking points: a professional working with them should be able to raise issues appropriately and be prepared to differ honestly and openly as well.

A professional who values self help groups accepts the need to make time to learn about them; sees the need for differing relationships with different groups, and makes sure they keep up to date, as they would with any area of professional expertise. They avoid using groups as a dumping ground for problems they would prefer not to face, because they know what groups can and can't do. They clarify issues to colleagues and support self help groups in public.

Respecting autonomy and confidentiality

A professional who wants to work with self help groups effectively understands and sees the implication of differences between professionally-run support groups and self help groups run by their members. They appreciate the correct professional role at any one time and the need to stay within it – or to change it. A competent professional accepts that members, not outsiders, make decisions about their group and understands the difference between raising issues, asking questions and offering support, all of which may be appropriate and valued by the group, and interference.

They see that a professional should not 'use' a group for purposes they don't want to be used for. They are aware of the risks of diverting scarce energy and time into pursuing a professionally set agenda, with the result that group members don't have time for all the matters on their own agenda.

A competent professional understands the many issues of confidentiality concerning individuals and the group: personal information as people talk in group meetings; information about members known to the professional but not group members; when the use of full names is inappropriate; and sometimes addresses of meeting places. They incorporate such confidentiality into the way they work and also clarify the degree of confidentiality which can be offered by their agency, making sure this is kept to by everyone working there.

A little goes a long way

A professional who has learnt to work with self help groups knows that a little can go a long way. Interest and knowledge does not necessarily mean involvement; support does not necessarily require attendance at meetings; providing too much information may prevent individuals taking action for themselves.

A competent professional is aware of a number of risks. If too much support is given, too leading a role taken, then there is a risk of the group being colonised and remaining as part of the professional system. Too close a physical presence – attendance at meetings or the group holding its meetings in a professional agency – may mean the group does not grow enough in confidence to run themselves. Too much help may mean they fail to develop self reliance and acquire skills. Too much involvement can mean that the distance required for creative criticism is absent and that creative tension is suppressed rather than being a step to useful change. A professional who puts people in touch with a group too enthusiastically can either scare someone off or make them feel they ought to go.

The general principles a competent professional works to are lightness of touch and the least degree of involvement possible in any given situation.

Opportunities for interaction

Successful working relationships, the competent professional knows, are enhanced by personal contact and interaction. They take opportunities that arise and create situations where self help groups and professionals can meet each other face to face. They especially value situations which give the chance to meet on neutral ground, allowing professional power to be less of an issue and self-helpers to be more confident.

A competent professional who wants to get to know a group does not always wait to be invited, but asks if they may pay a visit while knowing that being at an actual group meeting may not be the appropriate way to meet. They are aware of opportunities for self-helpers to visit professional agencies but take trouble to make visits as welcoming as possible and make it clear that their time and expertise is valued.

Their skill is not only in creating the chance for professionals and groups to meet, but in taking opportunities for potential members to meet people currently active in the group.

The competent professional keeps an eye open for group news in their local community – the local paper, radio, posters in public buildings – and anything written in newspapers and journals. They display material in their agency knowing that interaction is not always face to face. At times though, it may be the only way to deal with difficulties. The competent professional does not sit in silence or issue formal letters when an informal conversation might resolve what seems to be a problem. If needed, they seek out the help of an intermediary trusted by both sides.

Built into the bricks

Both agencies and individuals who are proficient in this area make sure that working with self help groups is built into every-day work and into operational systems. Agencies appointing staff include the topic and knowledge of relevant groups in to induction programmes and make sure their workers have access to accurate information. Conditions of service recognise the need to approve time-off-in-lieu for out of hours working. Supervision arrangements give the opportunity for support. Staff know they are expected to put people in touch with self help groups as part of agency policies and procedures.

Individual workers familiarise themselves with relevant groups as part of mapping community resources, and get to know about central sources of information about them before it might be needed. They exchange information with colleagues, informally and through using existing mechanisms.

Purchasers, policy makers and politicians build requirements and options for working with self help groups into plans and contracts and devise ways of measuring these which suit self help groups.

A mutual exchange

Investing time and resources which will benefit the group will be more than repaid. Both sides will gain.

"I don't know loads of things – Ruth tells me how to cope with certain kinds of situations. She's very good – you can get advice on anything."

(Kaneez, Asian Single Parents group)

"I don't attend the group. I've talked to them for mutual help and advice – I ask the leader for advice on problems I'm coming across, she might ask me to recommend speakers." *(Ruth, Social Worker)*

A competent professional is aware that both can benefit when the relationship works well: the group gains advantages; the professional and their organisation benefits. Individuals who are in need get more help and on the policy and planning level, group involvement in decision making is likely to help planners and purchasers create better services.

The professional's work is helped by the presence of an alternative or complementary form of help, enabling more professional time to be used for the work for which they were trained. The skilled professional is aware that sometimes use of professional services can be prevented and distress and isolation avoided. Good working relationships with groups are likely to result in a group encouraging someone in need to return to or ask for professional help. Knowledge by a professional about how to live with a problem increases through links with self help groups.

A professional seeking to develop their skills in working with self help groups does this not only in the context of their day to day work, but sees this as a way of enriching the whole work of an agency and professional services generally. Research projects and constructive feedback from groups on services contribute to growth in understanding and help change to take place.

A group benefits from the interest of competent professionals through gaining more members, getting access to information and resources and generally growing in self esteem, as a group and as individuals.

People not already members of groups but who might benefit from joining get help which they are unlikely to know about without information from professionals. The professional who puts people in touch with groups sees this as expanding the help a person can get, rather than limiting what is on offer to services provided by the professional world.

No automatic gain

While everyone can benefit, it is not a business relationship. Expecting a formal arrangement of mutual help between self help groups and professionals is not appropriate. Instead, a competent professional will see the relationship, if working well, as a series of mutually helpful exchanges. They know that the benefit may come through advantages which can't easily be measured, rather than expecting tangible services and quantifiable outcomes.

A competent professional makes sure the benefit is mutual. Self help groups are not there just to be useful to professional agencies. Expecting a group to fill a gap by providing services which should be part of good publicly funded and provided care is not acceptable. There can be a risk in overdoing requests made to a group. The principle of mutual benefit may be right as part of the foundation of the relationship, but not to the extent that the powerful professional world becomes the winner at the expense of the small self help group. The challenge to the professional world of today is to learn, change, and take action, without doing too much, or distorting or over-formalising largely informal community initiatives. Both self help groups and professionals can gain – the ultimate goal is growth for both.

References and further reading

Adams, R (1990) *Self-help, social work and empowerment*, Macmillan/BASW.

Agbalaya, F (1993) *Black People and Self Help*, Manchester Self Help Resource Centre.

Audit Commission (1993) *What seems to be the matter: communications between hospitals and patients*, HMSO.

Borkman, T (1990) in Powell.

Chesler, M (1990) in Powell, p 320.

Douglas, T (1978) *Basic Groupwork*, Tavistock Publications.

Drennan, V (1988) *Health visitors and groups: politics and practice*, Heinemann Nursing, p 118, p 119 and other references.

Emrick, CD (1987) "Alcoholics Anonymous: affiliation processes and effectiveness as treatment", *Alcoholism: clinical and experimental research*, Vol II, No 5, September/October pp 416–23.

Evans, L, Forder, A, Ward, L and Clarke, I (1986) *Working with parents of handicapped children – a guide to self help groups and casework with families*, Bedford Square Press.

Farquharson, A (1990) in Romeder, p 119.

Fielding, N (1990) "Black carers", *Community Care* , 11 January.

Haggard, L (1993) in *Care in the Community: the Self Help Option*, Report on the Derby Self Help Conference, 4 June, Derby CVS.

Hatch, S and Hinton, T (1986) *Self-help in practice: a study of Contact a Family, community work and family support*, University of Sheffield, Joint Unit for Social Services Research.

159

Hills, N, Staines, M and Stern, E (1988) *Self help in rural areas – is it different?* Report of Rural Research Group, COVAS Occasional Papers, Tavistock Institute of Human Relations.

Lavoie, F, Farquharson, A and Kennedy, M (1994) *Ethical issues in professional and self help group collaboration*, Université Laval, Quebec, Canada.

Lawyer, L, Macdonald-Lowson, S and Timmins, L (1989) *Changing places: from facilitator to support, a guide for women's mutual support groups*, Vancouver YWCA, 580, Burrard St., Vancouver, BC, Canada V6C 2K9.

Lindow, V (1994) *Self-help alternatives to mental health services*, Mind Publications.

Miller, E and Webb, B (1988) *The nature of effective self-help support in different contexts*, COVAS Occasional Paper No 3, Tavistock Institute of Human Relations.

Powell, T (ed.) (1990) *Working with self-help*, NASW Press, Silver Spring, MD.

Reading, P (1994) *Community care and the voluntary sector*, Venture Press, BASW.

Romeder, JM (1990) *The Self-Help Way: Mutual Aid and Health*, Canadian Council on Social Development.

Smiles, S (1958) *Self-help* (original publication), centenary edition, John Murray.

Sumner, Pat (1994) "Just the ticket", *Nursing Times*, 25 May, Vol 90, No 21, pp 50–51

Tavistock Institute of Human Relations (1989) *Self help support and black people*, COVAS Occasional Paper No 4, March.

The Self Help Team (1993–4) *A plan for the year.*

Trojan, A (1989) "Benefits of self help groups: a survey of 232 members from 65 disease–related groups", *Social Science and Medicine*, Vol 29, No 2, pp 225–32.

Wann, M (1995) *Building social capital: Self help in a twenty-first century welfare state*, Institute for Public Policy Research.

Williamson, C (1992) *Whose standards? Consumer and professional standards in health care*, Open University Press.

Wilson, J (1993) "Vital yet problematic: self help groups and professionals – a review of the literature in the last decade", *Health and Social Care in the Community*, 1: pp 211–18.

Wilson, J (1994a) *Good Links: guidelines for self help groups on working with professionals*, The Self Help Team, Nottingham.

Wilson, J (1994b) "Self help groups and professionals", *Findings, Social Care Research* 60, November, The Joseph Rowntree Foundation.

Wilson, J (1995) *Two Worlds: self help groups and professionals*, Venture Press, British Association of Social Workers.

Index